Welcome to zoom español 1

Abigail Hardwick
Isabel Alonso de Sudea
María Isabel Isern Vivanco

Meet Eva, José, Khalid and Marisa (in this book and on the *Zoom español* video).

Share their video blogs and find out more about them.

Symbols and headings you will find in the book: what do they mean?

 A video activity

 A listening activity

 A speaking activity

 A reading activity

 A writing activity

 Do this with a partner

 *Gramática* → p.162 Grammar information

 Think about this!

 Important words or phrases

 *Challenge* A challenge

Extra Star / Plus	Reinforcement and extension activities
Labolengua	Grammar, strategies, pronunciation
Prueba	Test yourself
Vocabulario	Unit vocabulary list
Leer	Reading pages
Gramática	Grammar reference
Glosario	Glossary

OXFORD
UNIVERSITY PRESS

Tabla de materias

¡Hola!

- Vocabulary: listen to some greetings
- Skills: practise the five vowel sounds; find out what you already know about Spain and Latin America

La Coruña
Oviedo
Santander
Bilbao
PAÍS VASCO
Pamplona
Francia
ASTURIAS
CANTABRIA
Vitoria
NAVARRA
Pirineos
GALICIA
Burgos
Vigo
CASTILLA-LEÓN
Logroño
LA RIOJA
Zaragoza
CATALUÑA
Valladolid
Barcelona
Salamanca
ARAGÓN
Menorca
Madrid
MADRID
España
Mallorca
Portugal
Cáceres
Toledo
Valencia
VALENCIA
Ibiza
BALEARES
Badajoz
CASTILLA-LA MANCHA
Formentera
EXTREMADURA
MURCIA
Córdoba
Murcia
La Palma
Sevilla
CANARIAS
Granada
Lanzarote
Cádiz
Tenerife
Fuerteventura
Málaga
Gran Canaria

España = 504.750 km²
Población = 46.661.950
Capital = Madrid

  Escucha y repite.
Listen and repeat.

¡Hola! ¿Qué tal? Soy Eva Hernández López de Barcelona.

Adiós por ahora de Khalid.

Me llamo José María Martín. ¡Hasta luego!

See Zoom OxBox

Saludos de Marisa García de Buenos Aires.

The five vowel sounds
a – e – i – o – u

🎧 **Listen and repeat these sounds.**
Practise pronouncing the countries making sure you use pure vowel sounds.

HABLAR 2 👥 **Pregunta y contesta.**
Ask and answer.

A ¿Cómo se llama la capital de ... ?
B Se llama ...

HABLAR 3 **¿Cuánto sabes ya?**
How much do you know already?

How many regions are there in Spain?
How many countries are there in Latin America?

How many islands make up the Canaries?
Name the islands in the Baleares.

Where are the Galapagos? Which country do they belong to?
Where is Easter Island? Which country owns it?

How many sports stars can you name from Spain? And Latin America? What sport do they play?

How many items of food or dishes can you name from Spain or Latin America?

Do you know the names of any dances from Spain or Latin America?

Challenge
Write down at least five things you know about Spain or Latin America.
Pool your ideas with the rest of the class and make up a quiz.
Find out more about one of the countries of Latin America.

Why do you think it is important to learn Spanish?

 *See Zoom OxBox*

Durante la clase

Vocabulary: understand classroom instructions

Escucha

Repite

Habla

Lee

Escribe

Pregunta

Indica

Contesta

Mira

Empareja

1 🎧 **Escucha y repite.**
Listen and repeat.

2 🎧 **Escucha e indica.**
Listen and point to the correct illustration.

3 👥 **¡Te toca a ti! Por turnos con tu compañero:**
It's your turn! Take turns with a partner:

Give an instruction. Your partner points it out.

4 👥 **¿Verdad o mentira? True or false?**
Give an instruction and an English meaning.
Your partner says if it is true or false.

⚙️ *Gramática* → p.164

Four ways to say 'you'

tú

vosotros

usted

ustedes

When you are giving instructions to
- one person informally use *tú*
- several people informally use *vosotros*
- one person formally use *usted*
- several people formally use *ustedes*

Work out which you would use when speaking to a friend's grandparents, a teacher, the head teacher, and the young brother of a friend.

The classroom instructions above are for one person – you informal.

See Zoom OxBox

Escucha y lee.
Listen and read. Which words or phrases can you guess the meaning of?

Empareja.
Match the English to the Spanish.

a How do you say ...
   in Spanish?
b How do you write it?
c I don't know.
d I don't understand.
e I haven't got a pen /
   pencil.
f May I borrow a pen?

g May I go to the toilet?
h Please.
i Thank you.
j What does ... mean
   in Spanish?
k What number is it?
l What page is it?

Challenge
Think of five more instructions or classroom phrases then look them up in a dictionary or ask your teacher for the Spanish. Put all your ideas together and make a poster for the classroom.

See Zoom OxBox

- Skills: learn some basic facts about Spanish-speaking people and culture; recognise and use greetings correctly

1 Completa el quiz: ¿A, B o C?
Do the quiz. Choose A, B or C.

Famosos
¿Quién es?

A	Raúl
B	Torres
C	Fàbregas

A	Jennifer Lopez
B	Shakira
C	Penélope Cruz

Monumentos
Se llama ...

A	La Costa del Sol
B	La Sagrada Familia
C	El Camp Nou

A	Machu Picchu
B	El Amazonas
C	El volcán de Popocatepetl

2 Escucha, lee y repite.
Listen, read and repeat the dialogues.

A

¡Hola! ¿Cómo te llamas?

Me llamo Abdul. ¿Y tú?

Me llamo Maribel.

B

Buenos días. ¿Qué tal?

Bien, ¿y tú?

Muy bien, gracias.

Adiós. Hasta pronto.

Buenos días

Buenas tardes

Buenas noches

See Zoom OxBox

Escucha otra vez.

Listen again. Find:

1 Greetings words/phrases
2 How to say 'My name is …'
3 How to ask 'What's your name?'
4 How to ask 'How are you?'
5 How to say 'Goodbye. See you soon.'

4 Practica el diálogo.
Practise the dialogue with a partner.

? Think

Look again at the dialogues. What do you notice about ! and ? Does this happen in English? Why do you think this happens in Spanish?

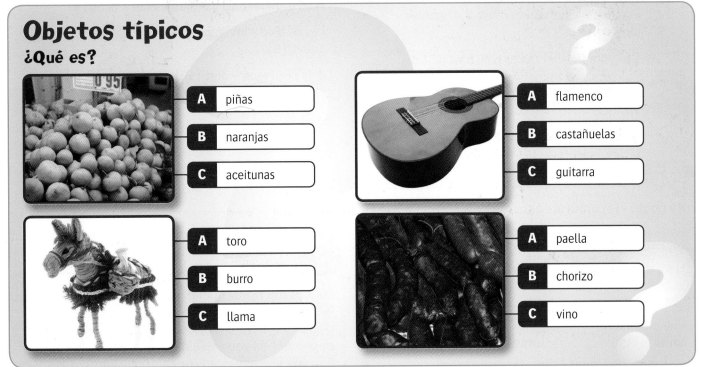

Challenge

Find out more about any three of the monuments or personalities you didn't choose as answers.

Objetos típicos

¿Qué es?

	A	piñas
	B	naranjas
	C	aceitunas

	A	flamenco
	B	castañuelas
	C	guitarra

	A	toro
	B	burro
	C	llama

	A	paella
	B	chorizo
	C	vino

Solución: Fábregas, B Shakira, A Machu Picchu, B naranjas, B burro, C guitarra, B chorizo

0.2 Me flipa; me molan

- Vocabulary: talk about things you like, using the alphabet
- Grammar: use definite and indefinite articles correctly; learn numbers 1–20
- Skills: record vocabulary accurately

A a B b C c D d   E e F f G g   H h I i J j K k   L l M m N n   Ñ ñ

O o P p Q q   R r S s T t U u   V v W w X x   Y y Z z

ESCUCHAR 1 🎧 **El abecedario español. Escucha y canta.**
Listen and do the rap.

ESCUCHAR 2 🎧 **Escucha y lee el poema.**
Listen to and read the poem.

How many letters sound like English letters?
Which ones are different?

LEER 3 **Lee las palabras.**
Study the words beginning with A–J and see how many you either know already or can guess because they are similar to English words.

HABLAR 4 👥 **Deletrea las palabras.**
Practise spelling them using the Spanish alphabet.

Can your partner guess which word it is?

ESCRIBIR 5 **Escribe las palabras que no sabes.**
Write down the words you simply do not know.

A es de **amigos** – es el número **uno** (1)

B es de **blog** – es el número **dos** (2)

C es de **CDs** – es el número **tres** (3)

D es de **discotecas** o **deporte** – es el número **cuatro** (4)

E es de **emails** o **emoticones** – es el número **cinco** (5)

F es de **fiestas** – **seis** (6)

G es de mis **grupos** favoritos – **siete** (7)

H es de **helados** y **hamburguesas** – **ocho** (8)

I es de **iPod** e **inventos** guay – **nueve** (9)

J es de **juegos** – **diez** (10)

⚙️ Gramática → p.162

All nouns in Spanish are either

masculine   or   feminine.
un helado   **una** hamburguesa

Here the word in Spanish for *a* or *an* which comes in front of the noun shows whether it is masculine or feminine.

The plural form *some* is
unos helados   **unas** hamburguesas

un/unos, una/unas (*a, an, some*) are called indefinite articles.

me flipa – *I love it*
me molan – *I'm into them*

❓ Think

Look at the words in the grammar box. Do the last letters (the endings) of these words help you to decide if the word is masculine or feminine, singular or plural? Can you explain this and make up a rule? Can you find any words on this page which don't follow this rule?

Escribe las palabras.
Now go back to your list from Activity 3 and write down if the words are masculine or feminine.

 Escribe las palabras.
Write down the masculine or feminine form for the words in your list from Activity 5.

Check your answers with a partner.

Escucha y repite.
Listen and repeat the numbers.

Juega con tu compañero.
A says a number. B names the object.

Escucha y lee el poema.
Listen and read the second part of the poem.

Once (11) es la letra **K** – es de **kitesurf**

Doce (12) es la letra **L** – es de **Los Simpson**

Trece (13) es la letra **M** – es de **móvil** y **música**

Catorce (14) es la letra **N** – es de **naranjas** y **¡no!**

Ñ es otra letra en el diccionario español

Quince (15) es la letra **O** – es de **osito**

Dieciséis (16) es la letra **P** – es de **pósters** y **películas**

Q es la letra que sigue y es difícil de ilustrar

Diecisiete (17) es la letra **R** – es de **revistas** y **regalos** y **la RR doble** es difícil de pronunciar

Dieciocho (18) es la letra **S** – es de **siesta** y **SMS**

Diecinueve (19) es la letra **T** – es de **tatuajes** y **Twitter**

Veinte (20) es la letra **U** – es de **universidad**

Para finalizar hay

la **V** de **vaqueros** y **videojuegos**

la **W** es de **windsurf** y **Wally** y la **Web**

la **X** es por los muchos besos que te quiero dar pero

la **Y** va sola porque no quiere bailar

Y la letra **Z** es de **zapatos** y **zumo** y **zzzzzzzzz** ...

 Gramática → p.162

Definite articles
In Spanish **el, la, los, las** meaning *the* also show you whether the word is masculine or feminine (the gender of the word) and they are placed in front, just like the indefinite articles.

	masculine	feminine
singular	el osito	la revista
plural	los ositos	las revistas

Plurals
To make a noun plural in Spanish you add an 's' if the word ends in a vowel. Add 'es' if the word ends in a consonant.

Examples:
emoticón – emoticones (no accent!)
móvil – móviles

Habla con tu compañero.

NC 2

A El número 12 es la letra L de Los Simpson.
B Sí. Correcto.
A El número 15 es la letra W de windsurf.
B No. Incorrecto.

Escribe las palabras.
Write out the words choosing the correct article.

1 un / una videojuego
2 las / los zapatos
3 un / una siesta
4 unos / unas regalos
5 un / una tatuaje

Challenge

Choose ten letters of the alphabet and find ten new words for your Spanish vocabulary list. Swap your list with a partner and see how many meanings you can guess.

Example: T es de **tele** *o* **tenis**.

- Vocabulary: talk about family members
- Grammar: learn and use the verbs *tener* and *ser*
- Skills: learn how to be an independent learner

Khalid

Marisa

la familia

los abuelos *grandparents*
el abuelo, la abuela *grandad, grandma*
los padres *parents*
el padre, la madre *father, mother*
el padrastro, la madrastra *step parents*
el marido (el esposo), la mujer
  (la esposa) *husband, wife*
los parientes *relatives*
el tío, la tía *uncle/Aunt*
el primo, la prima *cousin (m)-(f)*
los niños *children*
el hermano, la hermana *bro-sis*
el hermanastro, la hermanastra *step-siblings*
el hijo único, la hija única *only child (m)-(f)*
casado/a *married*
divorciado/a *divorced*

los nietos — grandchildren
el nieto (m)
la nieta (f)
zítane

¿Cuántas palabras conoces?
How many words from the vocabulary list can you guess?
Write down the English and add them to your vocabulary book.

Mira el video.
Watch the video and point out the family members in the vocabulary box each time they are mentioned.

Mira el video otra vez.
Watch, listen and check the note about Khalid's family.
Find two mistakes.

Khalid: padre Sudan; dos
hermanos Jorge y Elías;
hermana Sara; madre
JALAL profesora

Lee. ¿Quién es?
Read the speech bubble. Who is it?

> ¡Hola! Tengo un hermano pero no tengo hermanas.
> Mi hermano se llama Diego y mi madre es dentista.
> Me llamo ...?

Gramática → p.164

My name is	me llamo
His / Her name is	se llama
I've got / I have (a brother)	tengo (un hermano)
I haven't got (any sisters)	no tengo (hermanas)
I am	soy
he / she is	es

Escribe de ti.
NC 2
Write a speech bubble about yourself and your family.

 See Zoom OxBox

José

¿Verdad o mentira?
True or false?

1 Anita has two brothers.
2 Roberto is Jorge's grandfather.
3 Irene is Pepe's mother.
4 Amalia is Anita's sister.
5 Armando is José's uncle.

¿Quién eres?
Play a guessing game with your partner.

A Soy el padre de Jorge.
B Eres Armando.

Escribe la respuesta correcta.
Write down the correct answer in Spanish.

1 El hermano de mi madre es mi _____ .
2 Los padres de mi padre son mis _____ .
3 El hijo de mi tío es mi _____ .
4 Yo soy _____ de mi abuela.

Escucha y lee.

¡Hola, soy Tito! ¿Qué tal? Primero, **¿cómo te llamas – tu nombre completo?**

Pues me llamo María Magdalena López García.

¿Tienes hermanos?

Sí, tengo un hermano pero no tengo hermanas.

Y ¿cómo se llama tu hermano?

Se llama Diego.

¿Tienes abuelos?

Sí, se llaman Alberto y Beatriz.

Practica el diálogo.
Practise the dialogue with a partner.

Habla con tu compañero.

NC 2

Interview your partner using the questions in bold.

Gramática → p.166

llamarse	tener	ser
me llamo	tengo	soy
te llamas	tienes	eres
se llama	tiene	es
se llaman	tienen	son

Notice how the verb pattern changes according to the person. Look back at the grammar box on page 12 and work out how to say the following:
their names are; you are; he has

Challenge
Design an imaginary family tree and then play a guessing game using it.

NC 2

0.4 ¿Cuántos años tienes?

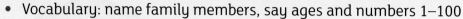

- Vocabulary: name family members, say ages and numbers 1–100
- Grammar: recycle language and verbs from the unit
- Skills: practise memory games – learn how to learn!

veintiuno 21 · **veintidós** 22 · **veintitrés** 23 · **veinticuatro** 24 · **veinticinco** 25 · **veintiséis** 26 · **veintisiete** 27 · **veintiocho** 28 · **veintinueve** 29 · **treinta** 30

Escucha e indica el número.
Listen and point to the number mentioned.

Escucha y anota los números.
Listen and note down the numbers. Which number comes next each time?

Practica. ¡Contrarreloj!
A says a number in Spanish. B says it back in English.
How fast can you go?

Ejemplo: **A** *el número ... veinticinco* **B** *number 25*

¿Cuántos años tienes?

NC 1

Look at the pictures and say how old you are.

Ejemplo:

Tengo trece años.

¿Cuántos años tienen?

NC 1–2

How old are they?
Write down each person's age.

13   14   12   15   10   11

Ejemplo: Susana tiene quince años.

Think

Watch out for the written accents!
Where do they come?
Learn them carefully.

See Zoom OxBox

30 = treinta	70 = setenta
40 = cuarenta	80 = ochenta
50 = cincuenta	90 = noventa
60 = sesenta	100 = cien

 **Think**

Can you relate these to the numbers 3–9?

Remember:
Numbers 31 onwards use *y* to join the numbers –
treinta y uno, treinta y dos, treinta y tres etc.

What do you think *y* means?

 Escucha y repite los números.
Listen and repeat the numbers.

 Escucha y anota los nombres y las edades.
NC 1–2
Look at the family tree on page 13 again.
Listen and note down their name and ages.

> 12 52 38 88 90

 Lee y completa la conversación.
Read the conversation and complete it with the correct words from the box.

¡Hola, Patricia! ¿Qué **(1)**?

¡Saludos! ¿Eres hija **(2)** o tienes hermanos?

Tengo una **(3)** y tres **(4)**. ¿Y tú?

Solamente tengo **(5)** hermano.

¿Tienes abuelos?

Sí, tengo una abuela y dos **(6)**.

Pues, yo no tengo **(7)** pero tengo tíos y una prima y tres **(8)**.

> abuelos (x2) hermana primos tal única hermanos un

 Escucha y verifica.
Listen and check your answers.

 Practica el diálogo.
Practise the dialogue with a partner.

 **Challenge**
Write down the names and ages of your own family members, or those of the family on page 13.

NC 2

 *See Zoom OxBox*

0.5 ⟫⟫ Gente y números ⟫⟫

- Vocabulary: use the vocabulary of this unit in a wider context
- Grammar: revise and extend the grammar you have learnt
- Skills: reinforce the skills you have learnt

ESCUCHAR 1 🎧 **Escucha y anota. ¿Cómo se escribe?**
Listen and note how it is spelt.

HABLAR 2 👥 **Deletrea los nombres.**
NC 1
Spell out the names. Take turns to guess which one it is.

1 Cesc Fàbregas
2 Penélope Cruz
3 Shakira
4 Lionel Messi

> If there is an accent on a letter, you say 'con acento escrito'.

LEER 3 **Mira las páginas 10 y 11 otra vez. Lee las frases. ¿Correcto o incorrecto?**
Look back at pages 10 and 11. Read the statements.
Decide if they are right or wrong.

Ejemplo: El número doce es la letra L. Correcto.

1 El número cuatro es la letra D.
2 El número cinco es la letra C.
3 El número diez es la letra J.

4 El número dieciséis es la letra Q.
5 El número veintidós es la letra Z.

HABLAR 4 **Corrige las frases incorrectas.**
Correct the incorrect statements.

ESCRIBIR 5 **Escribe: ¿Cuántos hay?**
NC 2
Write down how many there are.

Ejemplo: a Hay tres ositos.

> hay = *there is / there are*

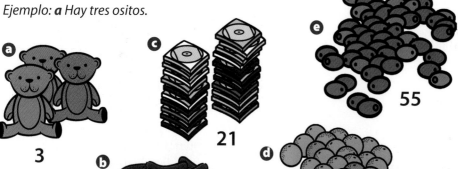

3

14

21

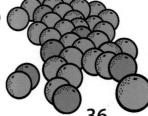

36

55

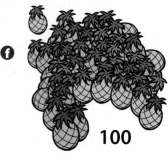

100

See Zoom OxBox

Escucha y lee.

Listen and read the conversation about Roberto's family.

> Tengo tres abuelos – dos abuelos y una abuela.
>
> ¿Cómo se llaman?
>
> Se llaman Alfredo, Mario y Fernanda.
>
> ¿Cuántos años tienen?
>
> Alfredo tiene ochenta y dos años; Mario tiene setenta y nueve y Fernanda tiene sesenta y siete nada más.
>
> ¿Tienes primos?
>
> Sí, tengo un primo y tres primas.
>
> ¿Tienes hermanos?
>
> Pues, no tengo hermanos, soy hijo único pero tengo dos hermanastras.

  Inventa un diálogo similar.

Invent a similar dialogue with a partner.

NC 2–3

 Dibuja el árbol genealógico de Roberto.

Draw as much of Roberto's family tree as you can.

NC 2

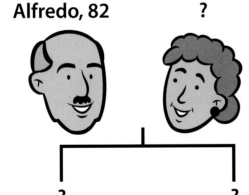

Alfredo, 82　　　**?**

?　　　　　**?**

 Escucha y completa el árbol.

Now listen and complete the family tree.

NC 3–4

Alberto	Julia
Alicia	Mariana
Cecilia	Paco
Enrique	

 Contesta a las preguntas.

Answer the questions.

NC 4

Ejemplo: 1 Sí, (tiene un hijo que se llama Alberto).

1 ¿Alfredo tiene un hijo?
2 ¿Fernanda es la esposa de Mario?
3 ¿Paco es el primo de Roberto?
4 ¿Julia es la hermana de Cecilia?
5 ¿Cuántos primos tiene Roberto en total?

Comprender – Nouns, gender and verbs

A Nouns

Remember the little words (*the, a, an, some*) in front of the noun show you if it is masculine or feminine.

	singular			plural	
	masculine	feminine		masculine	feminine
a, an	un	una	*some*	unos	unas (*indefinite articles*)
the	el	la		los	las (*definite articles*)

There is another way to check the gender of a noun in Spanish. Many nouns ending in **o** are masculine and many ending in **a** are feminine.

How many words have you come across so far which do not end in an o or an a? Make a list of them and learn their gender carefully.

> **What are nouns?**

> Nouns are words used to name people, animals, places, objects and ideas.

> **What does 'gender' mean?**

> All Spanish nouns are either masculine or feminine. The term 'gender' is used to show whether the word belongs to the masculine group or the feminine group.

B Verbs

A verb tells you what is happening in a sentence. Most verbs follow a regular pattern – **regular** verbs. Some do not – **irregular** verbs.

In this opening unit you have only come across three verbs:

llamar(se) *to be called,* tener *to have,* ser *to be.*

When you look up a verb in the dictionary you will find it in the **infinitive** form as shown in the verbs above.

Spanish verbs fall into three groups: -**ar**, -**er** and -**ir**. The last two letters of the infinitive show you which group the verb belongs to.

The endings of the verbs in Spanish change according to the person (*I, you, he, she, we, they*) or thing (*it*) doing the action. This means you don't need to include the person unless you want to emphasise who is doing the action.

llamarse – *to be called*	tener – *to have*	ser – *to be*
(yo) me llamo – *I call myself = I am called (my name is)*	tengo	soy
	tienes	eres
	tiene	es
	tenemos	somos
(tú) te llamas	tenéis	sois
(él / ella) se llama	tienen	son
(nosotros) nos llamamos		
(vosotros) os llamáis		
(ellos) se llaman		

1 Do you remember these words? Are they masculine or feminine?

Write them using *un, una, unos, unas.*

Example: una naranja

1 naranja
2 videojuego
3 guitarra
4 burro
5 tatuaje
6 email
7 póster
8 chorizo

Now check them in the glossary at the back of this book.

2 Explain how you make the plural of words which end in a consonant.

3 Write out the verbs on learning cards and add the person doing the action in brackets.

See Zoom OxBox

Aprender – Ways to record vocabulary

C Nouns
- **Always** make sure you know whether a noun is masculine or feminine.
- Colour code nouns, e.g. red for masculine, blue for feminine.
- Always write the gender.
- Make a clear division between Spanish and English.
- Make out special cards for words which break the rules.

un / el helado
una / la hamburguesa

4 Check your partner has recorded his/her vocabulary correctly.

D Verbs
- Write the whole verb out on a card. (Write the meaning in English on the back.)
- Put the cards into envelopes marked regular -ar, -er, -ir verbs and irregular verbs.

5 Write the persons, stem and endings for a verb onto small bits of paper. Place them in a box or envelope. Take out bits and match them up until you have the complete verb again.

E How to learn new words
- Words have **meanings**, **spellings** and **sounds** and you need to learn all three of these together.
- One simple rule is: **read**, **say**, **cover**, **write** then **check**.
- Write new words in groups and add to them as you meet more related words.
- Make up word webs with the key word in the middle.

6 Complete the word web for *la familia*.

Discuss these strategies for learning and see if you can come up with some more helpful ideas.

Hablar – Pronunciation

Vowels
The five vowel sounds are: a – e – i – o – u.

7 🎧 Listen to the pure sounds and repeat them.

8 Stand in front of a mirror and look at the shape of your mouth as you pronounce each vowel.

9 🎧 Now listen and repeat these names.

Ana, Armando
Enrique, Elena
Isidoro, Irene
Oswaldo, Olguita
Umberto, Ursula

10 Practise with words from pages 10 and 11.

See Zoom OxBox

- **Skills:** practise spelling names; practise saying numbers; give personal information

HABLAR 1

Deletrea los nombres.
Spell out the names then check your answers against the alphabet on page 10.

1 R-O-B-E-R-T-O
2 M-A-R-I-E-L-E-N-A
3 A-L-F-R-E-D-O
4 L-O-R-E-N-A
5 J-A-V-I-E-R

LEER 2

Busca las palabras.
How many words can you find in the snake?
Look back at page 9 first.

heladochorizovinopiñavaquerosositomadreprimasabuelos

HABLAR 3

NC 1

Di los números.
Time yourself. How fast can you say these numbers?

3   6   21   50   34

12   15   65   100

HABLAR 4

NC 1–2

👥 **Practica el diálogo.**
Practise the dialogue.

¡Hola! ¿Qué tal?
¡Hola! ¿Cómo te llamas?
Me llamo ... . Y tú, ¿cómo te llamas?

Me llamo ...
¿Cuánto años tienes?
Tengo ... años. Y tú, ¿cuántos tienes?
Tengo ...

See Zoom OxBox

- Skills: understand information about people's families; give details about your own family

LEER 1

NC 2

Empareja las preguntas con las respuestas.

1 ¿Cómo te llamas?
2 ¿Cuánto años tienes?
3 ¿Tienes hermanos?
4 ¿Tienes abuelos?
5 ¿Cómo se llaman?

a No, no tengo hermanos; soy hijo único.
b Se llaman Clara, Rafael y José.
c Me llamo ...
d Sí, tengo tres abuelos.
e Tengo ... años.

ESCUCHAR 2

NC 2–3

🎧 **Escucha y anota los nombres de cada familia.**

Ejemplo: Cecilia has ...

Cecilia   Diego   Susana   Enrique

ESCUCHAR 3

NC 2

🎧 **Escucha otra vez e identifica a la familia.**

VIDEO 4

NC 3

🎥 **Mira el video-blog. ¿Cómo contestan a las preguntas?**

- ¿Tienes hermanos o hermanas?
- ¿Cuántas personas hay en tu familia?
- ¿Cómo se llaman?
- ¿Cuántos años tienen?

ESCRIBIR 5

NC 2

Contesta a las preguntas sobre ti.

See Zoom OxBox

🎧 Escuchar

NC 2

Listen to these six people. What are they talking about?

Example: 1 e

a age
b country
c brother
d favourite thing
e grandparents
f parents

Hablar

NC 1–2

Practise spelling out five names.

Example: C–E–C–I–L–I–A = Cecilia

Think of five countries and name the capital of each.

Example: Colombia = Bogotá

Leer

NC 1–2

Read and choose the correct word.

Example: 1 tienes

1 ¿Cuántos años tienes / tengo?
2 ¿Cómo / cuánto te llamas?
3 Mis abuelos se / me llaman Luis y Pacha.
4 Tengo dos hermanos / hermana.
5 María tiene una / un abuela.
6 Los / Las padres de Amalia se llaman Pepe y Nuria.

Escribir

NC 2–3

Write the answers to these questions in full sentences.

1 ¿Cómo se llama la capital de Colombia?
2 ¿Cuántos años tienes?
3 ¿Cómo te llamas?
4 ¿Tienes hermanos?
5 ¿Cómo se llaman tus padres?

See Zoom OxBox

¡Hola! / Hello!

¡Hola! — *Hello!*

Saludos — *Greetings*

¡Hola!	*Hello!*
Adiós	*Goodbye*
Hasta luego	*See you later*
Hasta pronto	*See you soon*
Soy Ana	*I am Ana*
Me llamo Federico	*My name is Federico*

Durante la clase / In class

escucha	*listen*
repite	*repeat*
habla	*speak*
lee	*read*
escribe	*write*
pregunta	*ask*
indica	*point to*
contesta	*answer*
mira	*look*
empareja	*match*

Quiz / Quiz

¿Cómo te llamas?	*What's your name?*
Se llama Olivia	*Her name is Olivia*
¿Qué tal?	*How are you?*
Buenos días	*Good morning*
Buenas tardes	*Good afternoon*
Buenas noches	*Good night*

Me flipa; me molan / I love it; I'm into them

uno	*one*
dos	*two*
tres	*three*
cuatro	*four*
cinco	*five*
seis	*six*
siete	*seven*
ocho	*eight*
nueve	*nine*
diez	*ten*
once	*eleven*
doce	*twelve*
trece	*thirteen*
catorce	*fourteen*
quince	*fifteen*
dieciséis	*sixteen*
diecisiete	*seventeen*
dieciocho	*eighteen*
diecinueve	*nineteen*
veinte	*twenty*

La familia / The family

el abuelo	*grandfather*
la abuela	*grandmother*
los abuelos	*grandparents*
mi padre	*my father*
mi madre	*my mother*
mis padres	*my parents*
el hermano	*brother*
la hermana	*sister*
el tío	*uncle*
la tía	*aunt*
el primo	*cousin (m)*
la prima	*cousin (f)*
el hermanastro	*stepbrother*
la hermanastra	*stepsister*
el padrastro	*stepfather*
la madrastra	*stepmother*
Soy hijo único	*I'm an only child (m)*
Soy hija única	*I'm an only child (f)*

¿Cuántos años tienes? / How old are you?

Tengo X años	*I'm X years old*
treinta	*thirty*
cuarenta	*forty*
cincuenta	*fifty*
sesenta	*sixty*
setenta	*seventy*
ochenta	*eighty*
noventa	*ninety*
cien	*a hundred*

Gente y números / People and numbers

hay	*there is, there are*
no hay	*there isn't, there aren't*

I can ...

- count from 1 to 100
- greet people
- talk about family members
- say how old I am and how old my family members are
- use the verbs *llamarse*, *tener* and *ser*
- understand the different ways of saying 'you' in Spanish

- Vocabulary: say dates and birthdays
- Grammar: use possessives adjectives correctly
- Skills: recognise when not to use capital letters

enero

Los Reyes Magos

febrero

El Carnaval

marzo

Las Fallas, Valencia

abril

La Feria de abril, Sevilla

mayo

Cruces de mayo

junio

Las hogueras de San Juan, Alicante

julio

Los Sanfermines, Pamplona

agosto

La Tomatina, Buñol

septiembre

La Diada de Cataluña

octubre

Día de la Hispanidad

noviembre

Todos los Santos

diciembre

La Navidad

ESCUCHAR 1

🎧 **Escucha y repite.**
Listen and repeat the months of the year.

ESCUCHAR 2

🎧 **Anota el día y el mes.**
Listen and write the month and day(s) of these festivals.

Ejemplo: 1 6 de enero

LEER 3

Pon los días de la semana en el orden correcto.
Using the calendar on the right, put the days of the week in the correct order.

3 **martes**   6 viernes   7 **sábado**   2 lunes   1 **domingo** 5 jueves   4 miércoles

ESCUCHAR 4

🎧 **Escucha y verifica.**
Listen and check your answers.

enero

D	L	M	M	J	V	S
						1
2	3	4	5	6	7	8
9	10	11	12	13	14	15
16	17	18	19	20	21	22
23	24	25	26	27	28	29
30	31					

? **Think**

What do you notice about the way the months and days are spelled in Spanish?

 See Zoom OxBox

5 **Repaso: Decid los números 1–31 en voz alta.**
With a partner say the numbers from 1 to 31 out loud as fast as possible.

6 **Lee.**
Read the speech bubbles. What do they mean?

¿Cuándo es tu cumpleaños?

Mi cumpleaños es el catorce de febrero.

7 **Escribe las frases.**
Write sentences.

NC 2

Ejemplo: 7/12 – Mi cumpleaños es el siete de diciembre.

18/7   30/1   9/11   31/3   25/2   13/4

8 **Citas rápidas.**
NC 2
Speed-dating: Ask six of your classmates when their birthday is and note their answers.

¿Cuándo es tu cumpleaños?

Mi cumpleaños es el ...

Challenge

Translate these sentences into Spanish.

1. His birthday is the 3rd of March.
2. Our birthday is the 17th of July.
3. Your (singular) birthday is the 28th of January.
4. Her birthday is the 20th of September.
5. Their birthday is the 9th of June.

NC 2–3

9 **Mira los dibujos. ¿Cómo se dice ...?**
Look at the cartoons. How do you say ...?

Singular: my   your   his/her
Plural: our   your   their

Mi cumpleaños es el 3 de enero.

¿Cuándo es vuestro cumpleaños?

Nuestro cumpleaños es el 3 de enero.

Su cumpleaños es el 28 de agosto.

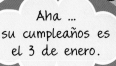

Aha ... su cumpleaños es el 3 de enero.

See Zoom OxBox

1A.2 Mis mascotas

- Vocabulary: say what pets you have and what colour they are
- Grammar: make adjectives agree correctly
- Skills: work out grammar rules from patterns

un ratón
un pájaro
un gato
una rata
una tortuga
un perro
una araña
un pez
un conejo
un caballo

Escucha y escribe.
Listen and write the correct animal in Spanish (1–10).

Ejemplo: 1 un gato

Escribe el singular.
Where do these plurals come from? Write the singular form.

Ejemplo: 1 un perro

1 dos perros	**3** cuatro ratones	**5** seis arañas
2 tres gatos	**4** cinco peces	**6** siete leones

Haz el plural.
Write out the plural of the animals in the house.

Ejemplo: 1 un gato – dos gatos (M)

Conversación.
Act out the conversation with a partner. Take it in turns to be A or B.

NC 2

? **Think**

Can you work out the rules to make the plural?
If a word ends in a vowel ...
If a word ends in a consonant ...

A ¿Tienes animales en casa?

B Sí, tengo

A ¿Cómo se llama(n) tu   / tu   / tus   ?

B Se llama(n) Boston / Isis / Snoopy y Pipo.

A ¿Cuántos años tiene(n)?

B Tiene(n)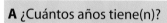

 See Zoom OxBox

En el Arca de Noé hay un elefante naranja, un tigre rojo, un gorila rosa, una jirafa gris, un hipopótamo negro, una tarántula verde, un cocodrilo amarillo, un camaleón azul, un delfín marrón, un canguro morado y un flamenco blanco.

 Think

What did you notice about Spanish adjectives (describing words) when you read the passage about Noah's Ark?

 Gramática → p.162

In Spanish all adjectives have a masculine form and a feminine form. We use the masculine to describe masculine nouns and the feminine to describe feminine nouns.

If the masc. ends in:	the feminine form:
-o	changes to -a
-l,- s, -e, or -n (except nationalities)	there is no change
-r	add an -a
-a (some exceptions like *rosa*)	there is no change

Remember you must also make them plural by adding an 's' or 'es' if the noun they describe is plural.

 LEER 5

¿Conoces los colores?

Do you know the Spanish colours? Use the text and picture above to work out 11 colours and their meaning.

 ESCRIBIR 6

Haz una tabla con los colores.

Complete the table with the colours in Activity 5.

	English	masc. sing.	fem. sing.	masc. pl.	fem. pl.
Example:	white	blanco	blanca	blancos	blancas

 ESCUCHAR 7

🎧 **Escucha y rellena la tabla (1–6).**

Listen and fill in the table.

	nombre	animal	cantidad	color
Example:	1 Jorge	perros	3	negros

Challenge

Ask five of your classmates about their pets by using the questions in Activity 4. Write out your findings.

Example: Catherine tiene tres perros marrones. Tienen dos, tres y once años y se llaman ...

NC 3

- Vocabulary: give your nationality and say what languages you speak
- Grammar: use the present tense of regular verbs
- Skills: pronounce Spanish 'c' correctly

Mira el video. ¿Cuál es la nacionalidad de Eva y Marisa? ¿Qué idiomas hablan?

What are Eva's and Marisa's nationalities?
And those of their parents?
What languages do they speak?
Watch the video.

Lee e identifica:
Read what these young people say and identify:

- three countries
- three nationalities
- five languages

a ¡Hola! Me llamo Paco. Soy colombiano pero vivo en España. Hablo español y catalán y aprendo inglés en el instituto.

b ¡Hola! Me llamo Amalia y soy guatemalteca. Vivo en Zacapa en Guatemala y hablo español y un poco de inglés. En el instituto aprendo francés.

Rellena la tabla.
Fill in the table, using a dictionary if necessary.

c ¿Qué tal? Me llamo Luís, soy paraguayo y vivo en Paraguay. Hablo guaraní y español y aprendo inglés en el instituto.

país	idioma	nacionalidad ♂	nacionalidad ♀
Soy de …	Hablo …	Soy …	Soy …
Vivo en …	Aprendo …		
Inglaterra	inglés	inglés	inglesa
Escocia		escocés	escocesa
Irlanda	irlandés		
Francia		francés	
			española
Alemania	alemán		
			italiana

¿Qué significan …?

NC 2

What do these verbs mean? Use them to write short sentences about yourself. Use the examples in Activity 2 to help you.

soy   vivo   hablo   aprendo

Think

Pronunciation

🎧 The letter **c** is pronounced like:
- k (**ka**yak) in front of a, o and u: capitán, concierto, curioso
- th (**th**eatre) in front of e and i: centro, cine

Listen, then practise pronouncing these words out loud:
cereal, cerámica, catástrofe, círculo, escocés, cámara, color, francés, ceremonia

See Zoom OxBox

5 Lee. ¿Qué pasó con *soy, vivo, hablo* y *aprendo*?
Read the speech bubble. What has happened
to *soy, vivo, hablo* and *aprendo*? Why?

Mi amiga se llama Amalia y es
guatemalteca. Vive en Zacapa
en Guatemala y habla español
y un poco de inglés. En el
instituto aprende francés.

Gramática → p.164

The present tense

Remember, a verb is a doing word like 'running', 'cooking' or 'dreaming'.

If you look up a verb in the dictionary you will find its infinitive form.

All Spanish infinitives end in **-ar**, **-er** or **-ir**. To help you remember we also
refer to the infinitive as the 'king' because it is the most important part of
a verb and it rules all others.

Pronombres personales (Who?)	Irregular		Regular			
	Ejemplo: **SER** *to be*		*Ejemplo:* **hablar** *(to speak)* –AR	*Ejemplo:* **aprender** *(to learn)* –ER	*Ejemplo:* **vivir** *(to live)* –IR
Singular yo *(I)*	soy		hablo	aprendo	vivo
Singular tú *(you)*	eres		hablas	aprendes	vives
Singular él/ella *(he/she)*	es		habla	aprende	vive
Plural nosotros/as *(we)*	somos		hablamos	aprendemos	vivimos
Plural vosotros/as *(you)*	sois		habláis	aprendéis	vivís
Plural ellos/as *(they)*	son		hablan	aprenden	viven

- Can you work out why *ser* is said to be **irregular**
while the others are **regular**?

- Think about your Spanish teacher. Can you write
a few sentences about him/her using the verbs
above? You may not need *aprender* (to learn) but
you can use *enseñar* (to teach) instead.

6 🎧 **Escucha y completa la información.**
Listen to these young people and fill in the information.
The first one has been done as an example.

Ejemplo: Se llama(n) _____Aurora_____   Vive(n) en ___Madrid, España___

Tiene(n) _____16 años_____   Habla(n) ___inglés y español___

Es/son _____americana_____   Aprende(n) _____francés_____

7 🎥 **Mira el video-blog. ¿Cómo contestan a las preguntas?**
Watch the video blog. How do they answer the questions?

- ¿Dónde vives?
- ¿Cuál es tu nacionalidad?
- ¿Qué idiomas hablas?

Challenge
👥 Ask a friend the
questions in Activity 7
and note their answers.
Then write a short
paragraph about them. NC 2–3

See Zoom OxBox

- Vocabulary: describe yourself and others
- Grammar: use quantifiers to enhance description
- Skills: extend sentences using simple connectives

Tengo el pelo rubio, largo y liso.

· EL PELO ·

① Pelo rubio, largo y rizado: 55€
② Pelo rubio, corto y liso: 25€
③ Pelo pelirrojo, largo y ondulado: 52€
④ Pelo pelirrojo, largo y rizado: 65€
⑤ Pelo castaño, largo y liso: 35€
⑥ Pelo castaño, corto y ondulado: 42€
⑦ Pelo negro, corto y rizado: 20€
⑧ Pelo negro, corto y de punta: 23€

rubio
pelirrojo
castaño
largo
corto
liso
rizado
ondulado
de punta

Escucha y elige.
Listen to these customers. Which wig have they bought?

Ejemplo: a 4

¿Qué significa ...?
With the help of the wig shop, work out the English meaning of the words in the vocabulary box.

To say your hair is neither short nor long you say: **No** tengo el pelo **ni** largo **ni** corto.

¿Verdad o mentira?
Look at the dark room. Is it true or false? Correct the false sentences.

Ejemplo: 1 Mentira: Tengo los ojos verdes.

F **1** Tengo los ojos marrones.
T **2** Tengo los ojos negros.
F **3** Tengo los ojos verdes.
F **4** Tengo los ojos azules.
T **5** Tengo los ojos marrones.
F **6** Tengo los ojos grises.

LOS OJOS

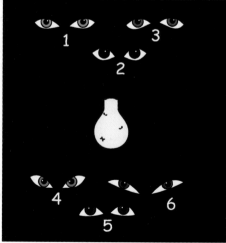

¿Cómo eres? ¡Descríbete!

NC 2

Use the vocabulary you have learnt on this page to write a short description of yourself.

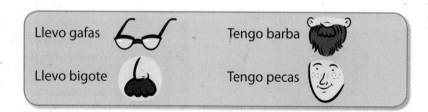

Llevo gafas

Tengo barba

Llevo bigote

Tengo pecas

See Zoom OxBox

LEER 5 ¿Qué dicen las chicas?
Look at what the boys say. What would the girls say?

Soy alto.

Soy gordo.

Soy bajo.

Soy delgado.

Soy alta.

No soy ni alto ni bajo, ni gordo ni delgado: soy de talla mediana.

LEER 6 Empareja los contrarios. ¿Qué significan?
Find the 8 pairs of opposite personality adjectives. What do they mean? Use a dictionary to help you.

ordenado/a
simpático/a
paciente
antipático/a
estudioso/a
testarudo/a
desordenado/a
impaciente
extrovertido/a
inteligente
tímido/a
flexible
bobo/a
maduro/a
inmaduro/a
perezoso/a

Gramática → p.168

Use quantifiers to extend your writing and reach a higher level:

demasiado	too
muy	very
bastante	quite
un poco	a little

ESCUCHAR 7 Escucha. ¿Es el chico a o el chico b?
Listen and decide who is being described. List the adjectives used.

ESCUCHAR 8 Describe al otro chico.
Describe the other boy.

NC 3

Challenge
Prepare a written description of one of your teachers. In small groups take it in turns to share your description out loud and work out who others have described.

Try using one or more of these connectives to extend your writing further:

pero	but
también	also
sin embargo	however

NC 2–3

 See Zoom OxBox

- Vocabulary: recognise words for additional animals, countries and nationalities

serpientes

toros

ovejas

vacas

cerdos

cobayas

patos

cabras

Escucha y verifica. ¿Qué falta?

Les is checking what animals he has on FarmSpace.
Which animals has he forgotten?

¡Traduce!

Translate!

NC 1–2

Ejemplo: 1 dos serpientes verdes

1 two green snakes
2 three black sheep
3 four white guinea pigs
4 five brown goats
5 six black and white cows
6 seven yellow ducks

Empareja.

Do you know the colours of these countries' flags?
Match each description to a flag.

Ejemplo: 1 a

país		bandera
1	Paquistán	verde y blanca
2	Marruecos	roja
3	Polonia	blanca y roja
4	Rumanía	azul, amarilla y roja
5	Senegal	verde, amarilla y roja
6	Somalia	azul y blanca
7	Turquía	roja y blanca
8	Estados Unidos	azul, blanca y roja
9	India	naranja, blanca y verde
10	Grecia	azul y blanca

See Zoom OxBox

Descifra y completa.
4 Work out the nationalities within the snake. Use them to complete
the table following the example.

paquistanípolacorumanomarroquísomalísenegalésgriegoestadounidenseturcoindio

Country *I am / we are* *from …* *I live / we live in …*	País *Soy / somos de …* *Vivo / vivimos* *en …*	Nationality (*I am / we are …*) / Nacionalidad			
		Soy …		Somos …	
		♂	♀	♂♂	♀♀
Pakistan	Paquistán	paquistaní	paquistaní	paquistanís	paquistanís
		polaco			

 ¡Bingo!
5 Bingo with a twist! Write nine nationalities you
NC 1–2 have learnt on these pages and pages 28 and
29. Take turns to call out a full sentence.

Ejemplo: Soy galesa.

Challenge

Write what these young people would say and
invent one other character. Pay attention to word
order and agreement.

*Example: Me llamo Layla, tengo trece años y mi
cumpleaños es el tres de enero. Vivo en España pero
soy marroquí. Hablo inglés y español y tengo tres
gatos negros.* **NC 2–3**

Comprender – Possessive adjectives and verbs

A Possessive adjectives

		Singular (one thing owned)	Plural (two or more things owned)
Singular (1 owner)	*my*	mi → mi perro	mis → mis perro**s**
	your	tu → tu perro	tus → tus perro**s**
	his/her/your (formal)	su → su perro	sus → sus perro**s**
Plural (2 or more owners)	*our*	nuestro → nuestr**o** perr**o** nuestra → nuestr**a** rat**a**	nuestros → nuestr**os** perr**os** nuestras → nuestr**as** rat**as**
	your	vuestro → vuestr**o** perr**o** vuestra → vuestr**a** rat**a**	vuestros → vuestr**os** perr**os** vuestras → vuestr**as** rat**as**
	their/your (formal)	su → su perro	sus → sus perro**s**

B Verbs – present tense

Pronombres personales (Who?)		Regular		
		−AR *Ejemplo:* cocin**ar** *(to cook)*	**−ER** *Ejemplo:* le**er** *(to read)*	**−IR** *Ejemplo:* escrib**ir** *(to write)*
Singular	yo	cocin**o**	le**o**	escrib**o**
	tú	cocin**as**	le**es**	escrib**es**
	él/ella	cocin**a**	le**e**	escrib**e**
Plural	nosotros/as	cocin**amos**	le**emos**	escrib**imos**
	vosotros/as	cocin**áis**	le**éis**	escrib**ís**
	ellos/as	cocin**an**	le**en**	escrib**en**

1 Add the correct possessive adjective.

Example: 1 mi

1 my rat → ▒▒▒ rata
2 his rabbit → ▒▒▒ conejo
3 your (plural) mother → ▒▒▒ ▒▒▒
4 my parents → ▒▒▒ padres

2 Look at this table and the table on page 29. Can you identify the pattern? Based on what you see, write rules to explain how regular verbs work.

3 Write in Spanish.

Example: 1 Beben Coca-Cola.

1 They drink coke.
2 We listen to rap music.
3 You (singular) teach French.
4 She calls her sister on the phone.

The multiple kingdoms of verbs

See Zoom OxBox

Aprender – Spelling, quantifiers and connectives

C Spelling

Remember, in Spanish it is a spelling error to use a capital letter for months of the year, days of the week, nationalities and languages unless these are at the beginning of a sentence.

4 Rewrite these sentences, correcting the errors where necessary.

*Example: 1 Vivo en Inglaterra pero soy **e**spañol.*

1 Vivo en Inglaterra pero soy Español.
2 Hoy es Martes tres de octubre.
3 Abril es mi mes favorito.
4 En Agosto visito a mis abuelos en Italia pero no hablo Italiano.

D Quantifiers and connectives

These help you improve the quality of your Spanish and achieve a higher level. Use them frequently to avoid short repetitive sentences.

un poco	a little	y	and
bastante	quite	pero	but
muy	very	también	also
demasiado	too	sin embargo	however

> Me llamo Phoebe. Soy americana. Vivo en Canadá. Soy alta. Soy delgada. Soy simpática. Soy estudiosa. Soy divertida. Tengo un perro. Es viejo. Es bobo. Es grande.

5 Improve Phoebe's work by rewriting what she says using quantifiers and connectives. You should use at least five different ones.

Hablar – Pronunciation

E Pronunciation – the letter c

The pronunciation of the letter c has the same pattern in Spanish as it does in English:

cat, **co**t and **cu**e but **ce**lery and **ci**nema

The correct way of pronouncing **ce** and **ci** in Spanish is like the 'th' in 'theatre'. However, in most Latin American countries and even in the South of Spain, people pronounce **ce** and **ci** almost like *se* and *si*.

6 Listen to these phrases. Which of the two boys is speaking? Pablo is South American, and Jordi is from Spain.

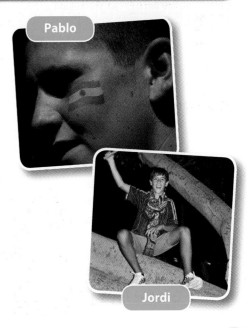

Pablo

Jordi

- Vocabulary: practise saying birthdays
- Skills: understand/give basic information about others

enero
10	Lewis Hamilton
16	Kate Moss
17	Muhammad Ali
21	Emma Bunton

febrero
2	Shakira
13	Robbie Williams
17	Paris Hilton
20	Rihanna

marzo
5	Eva Mendes
11	LeToya Luckett
20	Fernando Torres
24	Alyson Hannigan

abril
1	Susan Boyle
3	Leona Lewis
9	Kristen Stewart
13	Carlos Puyel

mayo
4	Cesc Fàbregas
8	Enrique Iglesias
13	Robert Pattinson
28	Kylie Minogue

junio
3	Rafael Nadal
4	Angelina Jolie
21	Príncipe William
30	Cheryl Cole

julio
3	Tom Cruise
17	Tash Hamilton
23	Daniel Radcliffe
29	Fernando Alonso

agosto
4	Barack Obama
16	Madonna
25	Alexandra Burke
29	Michael Jackson

septiembre
2	Salma Hayek
4	Beyoncé Knowles
6	Greg Rusedski
25	Will Smith

octubre
7	Simon Cowell
9	David Cameron
18	Zac Effron
20	Dannii Minogue

noviembre
7	Rio Ferdinand
8	Jack Osbourne
19	Calvin Klein
23	Miley Cyrus

diciembre
2	Britney Spears
18	Christina Aguilera
24	Ricky Martin
29	Jude Law

LEER 1 — **NC 2**

¿De quién se trata?
Who is it?

Ejemplo: 1 Britney Spears

1 Mi cumpleaños es el dos de diciembre.
2 Mi cumpleaños es el veintitrés de julio.
3 Mi cumpleaños es el cuatro de mayo.
4 Mi cumpleaños es el tres de junio.
5 Mi cumpleaños es el veinte de marzo.
6 Mi cumpleaños es el tres de abril.

LEER 2 — **NC 2**

¿De qué famoso del calendario se trata?
Who is it? Check on the calendar.

Ejemplo: 1 Fernando Torres

1 Soy futbolista y tengo 26 años. Soy español, pero hablo inglés y español. Mi cumpleaños es en marzo.
2 Tengo el pelo castaño y los ojos azules. No soy alta. Soy australiana y mi cumpleaños es en octubre.
3 Hablo italiano, español, inglés y portugués. Tengo el pelo largo y los ojos marrones. Soy colombiana pero vivo en Estados Unidos. Mi cumpleaños es en febrero.

ESCRIBIR 3 — **NC 3**

¡Tu turno!
Your turn: Choose two famous people from the calendar and write similar passages to the ones in Activity 2.

See Zoom OxBox

• Skills: revise the unit's vocabulary by reading information about others

LEER 1

NC 2

¿Qué se le preguntó?
What was she asked? Match the answers to the questions.

Ejemplo: **A** 7

A ¿Cómo te llamas?
B ¿Cuántos años tienes?
C ¿Cuándo es tu cumpleaños?
D ¿Cómo eres físicamente?
E ¿Cómo es tu personalidad?
F ¿Dónde vives?
G ¿Cuál es tu nacionalidad?
H ¿Qué idiomas hablas?
I ¿Tienes animales en casa?

1 Tengo el pelo largo y castaño y los ojos marrones. No soy alta, soy más bien baja.
2 Vivo en Londres en Inglaterra.
3 Hablo español, inglés y portugués.
4 Sí, tengo dos culebras verdes y un conejo blanco.
5 Soy simpática y habladora. Creo que soy generosa pero soy impaciente.
6 Es el veintiocho de diciembre.
7 Me llamo Cecilia.
8 Tengo dieciocho años.
9 Soy argentina, de Buenos Aires.

ESCRIBIR 2

NC 2–3

Escribe sobre Cecilia.
Write a paragraph about Cecilia using the information in Activity 1.
Remember to use the third person of the verb.

Ejemplo: Se llama Cecilia y tiene ...

LEER 3

NC 2–3

Problema de lógica.
Copy the table and fill it in by reading the sentences.

nombre	Ana	Marta	Rory	Freddie
Cumpleaños				
Descripción física			*alto*	
Personalidad			*impaciente*	
Nacionalidad				
Mascotas				

el chico
la chica
alguien

1 Rory es alto y no es paciente.
2 El cumpleaños de la chica rubia es el dos de marzo.
3 Marta cumple años el ocho de julio y es colombiana.
4 Un chico es extrovertido y tiene el pelo largo.
5 Un chico cumple años el trets de diciembre y el otro el quince de agosto.
6 Alguien es de Chile.
7 El cumpleaños de Freddie es antes que el cumpleaños de Rory.
8 La chica que no es rubia es simpática y tiene un conejo.
9 El chico impaciente es irlandés y tiene un tigre.
10 El escocés no tiene animales.
11 Dos personas no tienen animales en casa.
12 La rubia no tiene los ojos verdes y es traviesa.

See Zoom OxBox

1A.8 Prueba

1 Escuchar

NC 4

Listen and fill in the table.

name	Abdul-Wahid	Martha	Salvatore
Age	15		
Birthday	6/8		
Nationality	Moroccan		
Country	Spain		
Description	tall/quite slim		
Character	friendly/not studious		
Pets	black dog		
Extra	He is Khalid's friend		

2 Hablar

NC 2–4

Choose a picture and give your teacher as much information as you can about the person shown.

3 Leer

NC 3

Read the letters and write the name of the person each sentence refers to.

Example: 1 Shayne

1 His/her birthday is not in summer.
2 He/she has a silly pet.
3 He/she learns French in school.
4 He/she has brown hair.
5 He/she speaks a little German.
6 He/she is friendly.

4 Escribir

NC 3

Write three short sentences describing your best friend.

Málaga, 8 de agosto

¡Hola! Soy Sofía. El sábado celebré mi cumpleaños: ¡quince años! Soy italiana pero vivo en Málaga porque mi padre trabaja aquí. Se me dan bien los idiomas: hablo italiano, español y un poco de francés. En el instituto también estudio alemán así que lo hablo un poco. Soy alta y tengo el pelo castaño, largo y rizado. Soy bastante impaciente pero creo que soy muy simpática.

¡Hasta pronto!

Sofía

Barcelona, 26 de junio

¡Hola! Me llamo Shayne y mi mejor amigo es mi perro Coconut. Coconut es negro y tiene mucha energía pero es bastante bobo. Somos ingleses pero vivimos en Barcelona cerca de Marisa. Yo soy un poco testarudo pero soy estudioso. Físicamente soy delgado y tengo los ojos verdes. Por cierto, hablo inglés muy bien ¡claro! y español bastante bien, sin embargo en el instituto aprendo francés. ¡Ah! Mi cumpleaños es en Navidad. ¿Cuándo es tu cumpleaños?

¡Un abrazo!

Shayne

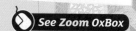
See Zoom OxBox

Cumpleaños y fiestas — *Birthdays and festivals*

enero	*January*
febrero	*February*
marzo	*March*
abril	*April*
mayo	*May*
junio	*June*
julio	*July*
agosto	*August*
septiembre	*September*
octubre	*October*
noviembre	*November*
diciembre	*December*
lunes	*Monday*
martes	*Tuesday*
miércoles	*Wednesday*
jueves	*Thursday*
viernes	*Friday*
sábado	*Saturday*
domingo	*Sunday*

Mis mascotas — *My pets*

un ratón	*a mouse*
un pájaro	*a bird*
un gato	*a cat*
una rata	*a rat*
una tortuga	*a turtle / tortoise*
un perro	*a dog*
una araña	*a spider*
un pez	*a fish*
un conejo	*a rabbit*
un caballo	*a horse*
una cobaya	*a guinea pig*
una serpiente	*a snake*
blanco/a	*white*
negro/a	*black*
rojo/a	*red*
azul	*blue*
verde	*green*
amarillo/a	*yellow*
naranja	*orange*
gris	*grey*
marrón	*brown*
rosa	*pink*
morado/a	*purple*

Lenguas y nacionalidades — *Languages and nationalities*

inglés/inglesa	*English*
escocés/escocesa	*Scottish*
irlandés/irlandesa	*Irish*
galés/galesa	*Welsh*
francés/francesa	*French*
español(a)	*Spanish*
portugués/portuguesa	*Portuguese*
italiano/a	*Italian*

¿Cómo eres? — *What are you like?*

Tengo ...	*I have ...*
el pelo	*hair*
largo	*long*
corto	*short*
liso	*straight*
rizado	*curly*
ondulado	*wavy*
de punta	*spiky*
los ojos	*eyes*
bigote	*moustache*
barba	*beard*
pecas	*freckles*
Llevo gafas	*I wear glasses*
Soy ...	*I am ...*
alto/a	*tall*
bajo/a	*short*
delgado/a	*slim*
gordo/a	*fat*
de talla mediana	*medium size*
ordenado/a	*tidy*
desordenado/a	*untidy*
simpático/a	*friendly*
antipático/a	*unfriendly*
paciente	*patient*
impaciente	*impatient*
estudioso/a	*studious*
perezoso/a	*lazy*
testarudo/a	*stubborn*
extrovertido/a	*outgoing*
tímido/a	*shy*
inteligente	*intelligent*
bobo/a	*silly*
maduro/a	*mature*
inmaduro/a	*immature*

⊚ I can ...

- ⊚ say when my birthday is and understand dates
- ⊚ say where I come from and my nationality
- ⊚ give a physical description of myself and others
- ⊚ give a personality description of myself and others
- ⊚ say what pets I have and their colours
- ⊚ use the present tense of regular verbs correctly
- ⊚ pronounce words with the letter **c** correctly

1B.1 Mis asignaturas

- Vocabulary: talk about school subjects and your opinions of them
- Grammar: use verbs and adjectival agreements correctly
- Skills: learn how to work out meaning from cognates

 LEER 1

👥 **Adivina las asignaturas.**

Work with a partner. How many subjects in the vocabulary box can you work out?

Ejemplo: el español = Spanish

 VIDEO 2

🎥 **Mira el video.**

Are the pictures above correct? Do Eva and José like and dislike the subjects shown?

Ejemplo: No, it's not correct. Eva likes English ...

 HABLAR 3

NC 2

👥 **Habla con tu compañero.**

Tell your partner which subjects you like and dislike. He/She makes notes.

Ejemplo: **A** *Me gusta el inglés.*
B *[writes] inglés* ♥

el español	la historia
el inglés	la informática
la educación física	la tecnología
la geografía	las ciencias
	las matemáticas

⚙️ *Gramática* → p.167

How to say you like or dislike something

me gusta mucho = ♥♥   no me gusta = ✖
me gusta = ♥   no me gusta nada = ✖✖

Careful!

Me gusta la historia. – *I like history. (singular – one thing)*
Me gust**an** las ciencias. – *I like sciences. (plural – more than one thing)*

▶ *See Zoom OxBox*

Rellena la tabla.

Listen to the students talking. Copy and complete the table.

	♥♥	♥	✗	✗✗
Cristina		*Ejemplo:* matemáticas		
Antonio				
Pedro				
Susana				

 **Think**

El inglés es aburrid**o**.
BUT
La geografía es aburrid**a**.
Why do you think the word endings are different?

La tecnología es interesant**e**.
BUT
Las matemáticas son interesant**es**.
Why do you think the word endings are different?

5 ¿Positivo o negativo?

Decide if these are positive (✓) or negative (✗) opinions about the subjects.

Ejemplo: La tecnología es bastante divertida. ✓

1 La historia es muy interesante.
2 Las matemáticas son muy útiles.
3 ¡La informática es demasiado difícil!
4 La educación física es muy fácil.
5 Las ciencias no son muy interesantes.
6 La geografía no es tan aburrida.

fácil	para mí
difícil	pero
útil	
aburrido/a	me gusta
divertido/a	te gusta
interesante	correcto
	mentira
un poco	
bastante	
tan	
muy	
demasiado	

 Escucha otra vez.

NC 2–3

Listen to Activity 4 again. Why do the students like or dislike the subjects?

 Escribe unas frases.

NC 3

Write down what you think about your school subjects.

Ejemplo: Para mí, el español es muy interesante, pero ...

 **Challenge**

Tell your friends what you think of a subject. Can they decide if you are telling the truth or not?

Example: **A** No me gusta nada el inglés, ¡es *tan* aburrido!
B ¡Mentira! Te gusta el inglés.
A Correcto – no digo la verdad. NC 2–3

 **See Zoom OxBox**

1B.2 La hora y el horario

- Vocabulary: say what time it is and when your lessons are
- Grammar: practise using the verb *tener*; use the verb *ser* with telling the time
- Skills: tell the time, transfer previous knowledge

a
Es la una.

b
Es la una y cinco.

c
Es la una y cuarto.

d
Es la una y veinte.

e
Es la una y media.

f
Son las dos menos veinticinco.

g
Son las dos menos cuarto.

h
Son las dos menos diez.

i
Son las dos.

 ESCUCHAR 1

🎧 **Identifica el reloj.**
Listen and decide which clock it is.

Ejemplo: 1 e

 LEER 2

Identifica el reloj.
Look at these clocks and match them to the sentences below.

1 Son las nueve y cuarto.
2 Son las siete y diez.
3 Son las seis y media.
4 Son las cinco menos cuarto.
5 Son las once.
6 Son las once menos cinco.

Ejemplo: 1 d

? Think

Es la una
BUT
Son las dos
Son las tres
Why do you think that is?

? Think

What do you think these mean?
Es el mediodía.

Es la medianoche.

 **See Zoom OxBox**

3 **Habla con tu compañero.**

Take it in turns to say a time. Your partner points to the correct clock on page 42.

4 **¿Verdad o mentira?**

Listen to Pablo talking about his timetable. Is what he's saying correct?

Ejemplo: 1 ✓

	lunes	martes	miércoles
9:00	matemáticas ☹	tecnología *¡Me chifla!*	ciencias *¡Qué horror!*
10:15	inglés	tecnología	ciencias
11:00		recreo	
11:15	geografía	matemáticas	inglés
12:00	ciencias	español	español
12:45		hora de comer	
14:45	informática	historia *muy aburrida*	deporte *¡Qué guay!*
15:30	español	inglés	deporte

correct clock on page 42.

Gramática → p.166

Remember:

tener – to have
tengo – I have
tienes – you have
tiene – he / she has
tenemos – we have
tenéis – you (plural) have
tienen – they have

---

es la una
son las dos
a la una
a las dos

---

5 **Identifica la asignatura.**

NC 2–3

Work with a partner. Say a day and a time. They have to work out which lesson you have then. Use Pablo's timetable.

Ejemplo: **A** *El lunes a las tres menos cuarto.*
B *Tienes informática.*
A *¡Correcto!*

6 **Copia y completa las frases.**

Complete the sentences with the correct part of the verb *tener*.

*Ejemplo: Carlos, ¿**tienes** historia el miércoles?*

1 María y yo _____ matemáticas a las once y cuarto.
2 Pablo _____ deporte el miércoles.
3 "Roberto y Elena, _____ español a las doce."
4 (Yo) _____ inglés el lunes, martes y miércoles.
5 Carmen _____ geografía a las once y cuarto.
6 Miguel, Martín y Ángel _____ tecnología el martes.

? **Think**

Where else would you use *tener*? Look back in the book.

Challenge

Draw out your own timetable. Personalise it by adding opinions as Pablo has done. Write a few sentences about it.

Example: El lunes a las nueve tengo historia. ¡Me gusta mucho!

NC 2–3

1B.3 Las instalaciones

- Vocabulary: talk about what there is in your school
- Grammar: use verbs correctly in the present tense; understand that subject pronouns are not much used in Spanish

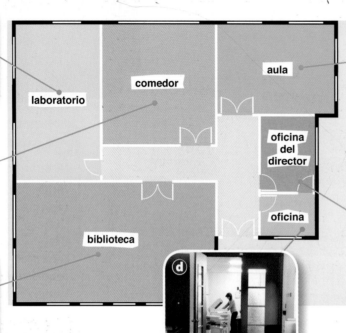

laboratorio

comedor

aula

oficina del director

patio

oficina

biblioteca

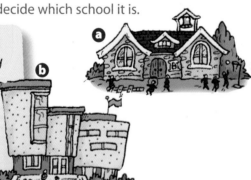

ESCUCHAR 1

🎧 **Escucha a Fernando.**
Listen and decide which part of the school it is.

Ejemplo: **1 f**

LEER 2

Lee la carta.
Read the description and decide which school it is.

el aula	grande
el gimnasio	pequeño/a
el laboratorio	moderno/a
el patio	antiguo/a
la biblioteca	bonito/a
la oficina	feo/a
la oficina del director	cómodo/a

Mi instituto es pequeño y antiguo. Hay un bonito patio y un comedor muy cómodo, pero no hay biblioteca. Hay unas aulas y un laboratorio. No hay gimnasio – practicamos deporte en el patio.

HABLAR 3

👥 **Juega con tu compañero o en grupo.**
Can you remember the places in the school?

NC 2

Ejemplo: **A** En mi instituto hay un gimnasio.
            B En mi instituto hay un gimnasio y una biblioteca ... etc.

⚙️ *Gramática*

hay – *there is / there are*

hay un comedor – *there is a canteen*

no hay biblioteca – *there isn't a library*

⊘ *See Zoom OxBox*

¿Quién?	¿Qué hace?	¿Dónde?
a I	**i** leer un libro 	**A** en la biblioteca
b you	**ii** comer un bocadillo	**B** en el laboratorio
c he / she	**iii** estudiar ciencias	**C** en el patio
d we	**iv** charlar con amigos	**D** en el comedor
e you (plural)	**v** practicar deporte	**E** en la oficina
f they	**vi** escribir cartas	**F** en el gimnasio

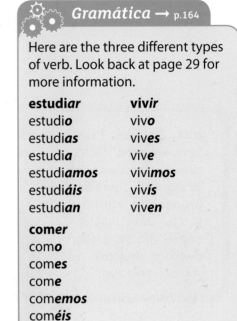

Gramática → p.164

Here are the three different types of verb. Look back at page 29 for more information.

estudiar	**vivir**
estudi**o**	viv**o**
estudi**as**	viv**es**
estudi**a**	viv**e**
estudi**amos**	viv**imos**
estudi**áis**	viv**ís**
estudi**an**	viv**en**

comer
com**o**
com**es**
com**e**
com**emos**
com**éis**
com**en**

LEER **4**

Lee las frases.
Find how the sentences are made up.

Ejemplo: Como un bocadillo en el comedor. = a, ii, D

1 Estudiamos ciencias en el laboratorio.
2 Juan y Roberto charlan con amigos en el patio.
3 María, ¿lees un libro en la biblioteca?
4 La secretaria escribe cartas en la oficina.
5 ¿Practicáis deporte en el gimnasio?

? **Think**

In Spanish, the words 'I', 'you', 'he', 'she' etc. are not used very much. How do you know who is doing the action?

ESCRIBIR **5**

Escribe la frase. ¿Es ridículo?
Write out these sentences using the grid. Do they make sense?

Ejemplo: Tomás c v B = Tomás practica deporte en el laboratorio. – ¡Es ridículo!

1 Paloma y Francisco f iv E
2 Sofía, ¿b iii B?
3 Trinidad y yo d v A
4 a v F
5 ¿e ii F?

leer un libro
comer un bocadillo
estudiar ciencias
charlar con amigos
practicar deporte
escribir cartas

Challenge

👥 With a partner, describe your school.

Take pictures of your school, label them in Spanish, and write about what you do in the different places.

Ejemplo: En mi instituto hay un gimnasio. Practicamos deporte. Me gusta mucho.

NC 2–3

1B.4 La ropa

- Vocabulary: talk about your school uniform and your opinion of it
- Grammar: use adjectives correctly
- Skills: develop ways of learning vocabulary

Hola, soy Sam. Para ir al instituto llevo uniforme. Llevo una camisa blanca, pantalones negros y un jersey azul. También llevo una corbata azul, amarilla y roja. Llevo zapatos negros. No me gusta mucho el uniforme, es práctico pero feo.

Hola, soy Carlos. Para ir al instituto llevo ropa cómoda – vaqueros y una camiseta, o un chándal y una camisa de fútbol. También llevo zapatillas de deporte. Me gusta mucho – es muy informal.

 ¿Sam o Carlos?
Listen and decide who it is.

Ejemplo: 1 Sam

 Mira el video-blog.
Watch Marisa, José and Khalid. What do they like/dislike about what they wear to school? Fill in a table like the one below.

	☺	☹
Marisa		
José		
Khalid		

 ¿Verdad o mentira?
Read the sentences about Sam and Carlos. Are they true?

Ejemplo: Sam lleva vaqueros. – Mentira.

1 Carlos lleva una camiseta.
2 Sam lleva una corbata.
3 Carlos lleva uniforme.
4 Sam lleva pantalones negros.
5 Carlos lleva un jersey azul.
6 Sam lleva zapatillas.

llevar	una falda
llevo ...	una sudadera
un chándal	unas zapatillas
un jersey	unos calcetines
un vestido	unos pantalones
una camisa	unos vaqueros
una camiseta	unos zapatos
una corbata	

? Think

Llevar is a regular verb like *hablar*.

How would you say *we wear shoes* or *they wear trousers*?

Gramática → p.162

Remember that adjectives agree with the noun they describe:
un**a** corbata negr**a**
un**os** zapatos negr**os**

 **See Zoom OxBox**

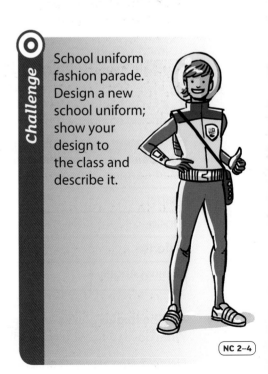

incómoda y fea

¿?

azul y amarilla

no me gusta

¿?

pantalones

una corbata

sábado y domingo

uniforme

ROPA

 Think

What other ways do you have of learning new words? Which works best for you?

incómodo/a	cómodo/a
elegante	feo/a
práctico/a	ridículo/a
formal	informal

ESCRIBIR
4
NC 1–2

Dibuja tu propio mapa mental.
Draw up a clothes mind map using clothes and opinions of your own.

HABLAR
5
NC 2

 Habla con tu compañero.
Play 20 questions with your partner. They think of an item of clothing from their mind map and you have to guess it.

Ejemplo: **A** ¿Llevas uniforme?
B Sí.
A ¿Llevas pantalones?
B No.
A ¿Llevas una camisa?
B Sí.

ESCUCHAR
6

 Escucha. Escoge el dibujo correcto.
Listen and choose the correct picture.

Ejemplo: 1 b

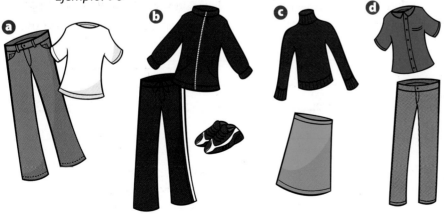

a b c d

Challenge
School uniform fashion parade. Design a new school uniform; show your design to the class and describe it.

NC 2–4

See Zoom OxBox

1B.5 »»> Me gusta ... »»>

- Vocabulary: learn the names for more school subjects, talk about patterns on clothes
- Grammar: use more adjectival agreements correctly

a el lenguaje

b la literatura

c el alemán

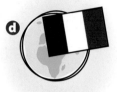
d el francés

e la religión

f la música

g el arte

h la ética

i la educación para la ciudadanía

LEER 1

Lee lo que opinan los estudiantes.
Read and note the subjects and if they like them or not.

Ejemplo: 1 b ✓

1. Mi asignatura favorita es la literatura española porque es muy interesante.
2. Me interesa el francés. Es bastante fácil.
3. ¿La religión? ¡Qué va! Y el profe es tan estricto también ...
4. La profesora de arte es muy simpática, pero ¡no me interesa nada!
5. ¿El alemán? ¡Ni hablar! Es demasiado difícil.

¡Ni hablar!
¡Qué va!
Me interesa(n) I'm interested
Me fascina(n) I'm fascinated
Mi asignatura preferida es ...
El/la profe es simpático/a
El/la profe es estricto/a
¿Qué opinas de ...?

ESCUCHAR 2

🎧 Escucha. Copia y completa la tabla.
Listen and complete the table.

nombre	asignatura	opinión	razón
Mari-Carmen	música	asignatura preferida	interesante, profe simpático
Isabel			
Rosita			
Alfonso			
Miguel Ángel			

ESCRIBIR 3

NC 3

Escribe lo que piensa tu compañero.
Write down what you think some of your friends would say about these subjects.

Ejemplo: La asignatura preferida de John es la música porque el profe es simpático.

See Zoom OxBox

 Escucha a los estudiantes.
Listen to the students and note down how well they are doing.

Ejemplo: **1** *c*

 Escribe tu opinión.
NC 2–3 Write down how well you think you are doing in different subjects.

Ejemplo: Soy bueno en inglés pero saco malas notas en ciencias.

 Escucha y anota la ropa.
Listen and note down the item of clothing.

Ejemplo: **1** *blue shirt with long sleeves*

 Juega al tres en raya.
NC 2 Play noughts and crosses with the grid below. Say what you are wearing to place your nought or cross.

Ejemplo: Llevo una camiseta con mangas cortas.

saco buenas notas
saco malas notas
soy bueno en ...
voy mal en ...
trabajo bien en ...
me esfuerzo en ...

a rayas
a flores
a cuadros
a puntos
sencillo/a
sin mangas
con mangas cortas
con mangas largas
con un logo

 **See Zoom OxBox**

Comprender – Adjectives and verbs

A Adjectival agreements

Adjectives describe a noun. In Spanish, the adjectives agree with the noun.

If the noun is masculine – *un perro* – the adjective must be too – *un perro gordo.*

If the noun is feminine – *la historia* – the adjective must agree with it – *la historia es aburrida.*

Most masculine nouns end in **o** and most feminine ones in **a**, but there are some exceptions. Look back through the book and see how many you can find.

If the noun is plural – *los pantalones* – the adjective must be plural too – *los pantalones verdes.*

1 Write sentences using the following nouns and adjectives. Remember to make them agree.

Ejemplo: gato / rojo
El gato no es rojo.

gato	falda	aulas	patios	inglés
rojo	corto	viejo	bonito	interesante

el profesor es simpátic**o**   m/s
la profesora es simpátic**a**   f/s
los profesores son simpátic**os**   m/pl
las profesoras son simpátic**as**   f/pl

Remember!
la camisa azul
las camisas azules

B Regular verbs

Verbs end in three ways in Spanish: *-ar (hablar), -er (comer), -ir (vivir).* Here are the endings for all three types of regular verbs.

	hablar	comer	vivir
yo	hablo	como	vivo
tú	hablas	comes	vives
él / ella / usted	habla	come	vive
nosotros	hablamos	comemos	vivimos
vosotros	habláis	coméis	vivís
ellos / ellas / ustedes	hablan	comen	viven

2 How would you say ... ?
   a María speaks Spanish.   **b** Marcos eats in the canteen.
   c Rafael lives in Madrid.

3 Transfer your skills. How would you say ... ?
   a We play sport. (*practicar*)   **b** You read a book. (*leer*)
   c They open their exercise books. (*abrir*)

4 Why are these sentences absurd?
   a Vivo en el comedor.   **b** Comemos unos pantalones negros.   **c** Hablan informática.

See Zoom OxBox

Aprender – Learning vocabulary

C Language learning tricks

Cognates are words that look similar in Spanish and English like *matemáticas, geografía, tecnología, interesante*. They can be very useful when learning new words.

5 Look back through the book. How many **cognates** can you find? Make a list.

> matemáticas,
> geografía,
> tecnología,
> interesante

Word association can also be helpful. *Simpático* means nice or friendly, but it looks like the English word 'sympathetic'. This can help you remember the meaning of the word, but **be careful** that you don't remember the wrong meaning!

6 What does this mean?
El instituto es grande.

  a The school is grand.   **b** The school is big.

7 Look back through the book again. Make a list of words that look similar to something in English but have a slightly different meaning.

In Spanish things are often said in a slightly different way. Remembering this can help you with unusual phrases. *Fuerte* means 'strong', but *Soy fuerte en matemáticas* means 'I am **good** at maths'. Draw pictures to help you remember phrases like this.

¿Un instituto grande?

Hablar – Pronunciation

D Pronunciation – emphasis

How do you know which part of the word to emphasise when speaking Spanish? It's easy!

1 If it has an accent, emphasise that syllable – geogra**fí**a, sim**pá**tico, mate**má**ticas.
2 If it ends in a **consonant** (but not **s** or **n**), emphasise the **last** syllable – Mad**rid**, co**mer**, a**zul**.
3 If it ends in a vowel, **s** or **n**, emphasise the **penultimate** (last but one) syllable – insti**tu**to, ca**mi**sas, **ha**blan, **vi**vo, abu**rri**da.

8 🎧 Where do you emphasise these words? Copy them and underline where you think the emphasis should go, then listen and check.

> practicar   falda   pantalones   inglés   comemos
> interesante

▶ **See Zoom OxBox**

- Vocabulary: practise telling the time
- Grammar: practise using *-ar* verbs
- Skills: work independently

LEER 1

NC 1–2

Escoge el dibujo y copia y completa la frase.
Match the sentences to the pictures. Copy and complete.

Ejemplo: 1 e Tengo informática a las cuatro menos cuarto.

1 Tengo español a ▨▨▨ .
2 Tengo geografía a ▨▨▨ .
3 Tengo matemáticas a ▨▨▨ .
4 Tengo deporte a ▨▨▨ .
5 Tengo ciencias a ▨▨▨ .

ESCRIBIR 2

NC 2–3

Mira tu horario.
Look at your own timetable. Write down when your lessons are.

Ejemplo: Tengo inglés a las dos y media el lunes.

ESCRIBIR 3

Copia y completa las frases.
Complete the sentences with the correct part of the verb *estudiar*.

*Ejemplo: Juan **estudia** francés el lunes a las diez y cuarto.*

1 Me gustan las lenguas. ▨▨▨ inglés el martes.
2 María y yo ▨▨▨ geografía a las diez el jueves.
3 Luis, ¿ ▨▨▨ el español a las once y media?
4 Marta ▨▨▨ historia a las tres menos cuarto.

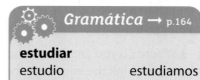

Gramática → p.164

estudiar

estudio	estudiamos
estudias	estudiáis
estudia	estudian

See Zoom OxBox

- Skills: understand how schools in Spain work; compare schools in different countries
- Grammar: understand *desde ... hasta ...*

¡Hola!
Me llamo Felipe y vivo en Madrid. Voy al Instituto de la Reina Isabel. Tengo clases desde las nueve de la mañana hasta las cinco de la tarde. Tenemos un recreo de quince minutos a las once. La hora de comer es a la una. Normalmente como en casa con mi familia. Tenemos clases otra vez a las tres. El miércoles tenemos deporte. Mi instituto es grande y moderno con muchas aulas, un gimnasio y un patio. Muchos profesores son simpáticos, pero hay unos profesores que son muy estrictos.

LEER 1

NC 3–4

Lee el correo electrónico.
Read the email and answer the questions.

1 What time does Felipe start school in the morning?
2 What time does he finish in the afternoon?
3 How long is his break?
4 What time is lunch?
5 Where does he eat lunch?
6 When do classes start again in the afternoon?
7 What does he do on Wednesday afternoon at school?
8 What is his school like?
9 What are the teachers like?

LEER 2

NC 3–4

¿Cómo se dice ...?
Find the Spanish for:

1 from 9 a.m. in the morning
2 till 5 p.m. in the afternoon
3 15 minutes long
4 normally
5 at home
6 on Wednesday
7 with
8 but
9 some
10 many

desde ... hasta ...
la mañana
la tarde

ESCRIBIR 3

NC 3

Escribe en español.
Using what you learnt in Activity 2, write these sentences in Spanish.

1 I have lessons from 9.30 in the morning.
2 We have a break 20 minutes long.
3 Normally I eat in the canteen.
4 Some teachers are funny.

ESCRIBIR 4

NC 3–4

Describe tu instituto.
Using Felipe's email as an example, describe your school and your school day.

 See Zoom OxBox

Escuchar

Escuchar

NC 3

Listen, copy and complete the timetable. Add a smiley or frowning face to show if Luisa likes each subject or not.

	lunes	opinión
8:30	matemáticas ☺	profe divertido
9:30	1	
10:30	recreo	
10:50	2	
11:50	3	
12:50	hora de comer	
14:15	4	
15:15	5	

Hablar

Hablar

NC 3

Choose one of these people. Imagine what their favourite subject is, and explain what they like and what they dislike and why.

Leer

Leer

NC 2–3

Read Eva's email and decide if the statements are true or false.

1 Eva has English four days a week.
2 She likes English.
3 She thinks geography is interesting.
4 She has geography on Friday at 2 p.m.
5 The maths teacher is very nice.
6 Eva thinks maths is difficult.

¿Qué tal tu horario? El mio está bastante bien. Tengo inglés el lunes, el martes, el miércoles, el jueves y el viernes – ¡es fantástico! ¡Me encanta el inglés! Es fácil y divertido. La geografía – pues, no me gusta mucho. Es bastante aburrida. Tengo geografía el martes a las dos. Pero la profesora de matemáticas es muy inteligente y simpática. Tenemos matemáticas el lunes, el martes y el jueves – es muy interesante.

Escribir

Escribir

NC 3–4

Describe this uniform.
What do you think of it?

Vocabulario

Mis asignaturas — *My subjects*

la educación física	PE
el español	Spanish
el inglés	English
la geografía	geography
la historia	history
la informática	ICT
la tecnología	design and technology
las ciencias	science
las matemáticas	mathematics
fácil	easy
difícil	difficult
útil	useful
aburrido/a	boring
divertido/a	fun, amusing
interesante	interesting
un poco	a little
bastante	fairly, quite
tan	so
muy	very
demasiado	too (much)
para mí	for me
pero	but
me gusta	I like
te gusta	you like
correcto	true
mentira	false

La hora y el horario — *Time and timetable*

Es la una	It is one o'clock.
... y cinco	... five past one
... y cuarto	... a quarter past one
... y veinte	... twenty past one
... y media	... half past one
Son las dos	It is two o'clock.
... menos veinticinco	... twenty-five to two
... menos cuarto	... a quarter to two
... menos diez	... ten to two
Es el mediodía	It is midday.
Es la medianoche	It is midnight.

Las instalaciones — *School buildings*

el aula	the classroom
el gimnasio	the gym
el laboratorio	the laboratory
el patio	the playground
la biblioteca	the library
la oficina	the office
la oficina del director	the headteacher's office
grande	large
pequeño/a	small
moderno/a	modern
antiguo/a	old
bonito/a	attractive
feo/a	ugly
cómodo/a	comfortable
hay	there is/there are
leer un libro	to read a book
comer un bocadillo	to eat a sandwich
estudiar ciencias	to study science
charlar con amigos	to chat with friends
practicar deporte	to play sport
escribir cartas	to write letters

La ropa — *Clothes*

llevar	to wear
un jersey	a jersey
una camisa	a shirt
una camiseta	a blouse
una corbata	a tie
una falda	a skirt
una sudadera	a sweatshirt
unas zapatillas	trainers
unos calcetines	socks
unos pantalones	trousers
unos vaqueros	jeans
unos zapatos	shoes
incómodo/a	uncomfortable
elegante	stylish
práctico/a	practical
formal	formal
feo/a	ugly
ridículo/a	ridiculous
informal	informal

I can ...

- talk about different school subjects and say what I think of them
- tell the time
- describe my timetable
- describe my school
- talk about uniform and clothes and give my opinion
- use regular verbs correctly

See Zoom OxBox

cincuenta y cinco **55**

2A.1 El tiempo

- Vocabulary: talk about the weather
- Grammar: use the radical-changing verb *jugar* (*ue*); recognise and use idioms with the verb *hacer*

 VIDEO 1 📹 **Mira el video.**
Watch the video and note when you hear the phrases opposite mentioned.

 ESCUCHAR 2 **Escucha, repite e identifica el dibujo.**
Listen to and repeat the phrases, then identify the correct picture.

 HABLAR 3 👥 **Habla con tu compañero.**
With your partner, say weather phrases and the letter of the picture below.

    A Hace sol.
    B Dibujo e.

 ⓐ
 ⓑ
 ⓒ

 ⓓ
 ⓔ

"Normalmente hace buen tiempo ..."

"Aquí no llueve muy a menudo ..."

Hace ...

1 buen tiempo
2 mal tiempo
3 frío
4 calor
5 sol
6 viento

Hay ...

7 tormenta
8 niebla
9 nubes

10 llueve
11 nieva

marzo abril mayo	junio julio agosto	septiembre octubre noviembre	diciembre enero febrero

La primavera	**El verano**	**El otoño**	**El invierno**

Las estaciones del año en Europa

❓ Think

The verb *hacer* is irregular and is used a lot – it means 'to do' or 'to make'.

Here it is used as a set phrase to describe weather conditions.

When you learnt to tell the time in Unit 1B you learnt set phrases which didn't translate literally from Spanish to English. This is called using idiomatic language.

Look at the phrases and symbols in the next column and say what they mean in English. Then translate them literally using the verb to do/to make and discuss the difference with your teacher.

 ESCRIBIR 4 NC 3 **Lee y escribe un texto similar.**
Choose another season and write a similar text.

> En primavera normalmente hace buen tiempo. En abril llueve pero en mayo hace calor y sol.

▶ **See Zoom OxBox**

ESCUCHAR 5

 Escucha. ¿Qué tiempo hace? ¿En qué día?
Listen and identify the weather on each day.

Ejemplo: **1** lunes

HABLAR 6

 Habla con tu compañero.
Ask your partner which sports he/she plays.

NC 2–3

A ¿Juegas al golf?
B No, no juego al golf pero sí juego al baloncesto.

> pero   también   sin embargo   en cambio

LEER 7

Lee el diálogo y contesta a las preguntas.
Read the dialogue and answer the questions.

José Me gusta jugar al fútbol.

Marisa ¿Juegas a menudo?

José Sí, juego todos los lunes.

Marisa Pues yo juego al tenis si hace buen tiempo, pero si llueve hago windsurf.

José Los sábados también juego al baloncesto con un equipo.

Marisa ¿Cómo se llama el equipo?

José Se llama Los Vampiros. ¡Somos bastante buenos!

Marisa ¡Qué bien!

1 Who plays tennis?
2 When does Marisa go windsurfing?
3 What happens on Mondays?

4 What is the name of the basketball team?
5 What does Marisa think about that?

Los diez deportes más populares de España

el fútbol	el atletismo
el golf	el boxeo
el baloncesto	la pelota vasca
el tenis	el windsurf
el ciclismo	el voleibol

Gramática → p.166

Radical-changing verbs

Some verbs change their spelling in all the persons except *nosotros* (we) and *vosotros* (you plural). The way they change is shown in the dictionary like this: *jugar (ue)*.

Jugar changes as follows:

juego	jugamos
juegas	jugáis
juega	**jue**gan

- Look at the pattern and learn where the changes are. It may help you to number the parts of the verb and call them '1236 verbs'.
- Can you write the personal pronouns for each part of the verb?
- Notice that you say *jugar a: juego al tenis, jugamos al fútbol*

Challenge

Write about what sports are played in each season.

List all the sports you can think of in Spanish under the following headings.

ball   combat   water
wheels   athletics

Choose four sports and write a sentence about when you would play each one (weather and season). Say why. **NC 2–3**

 See Zoom OxBox

- Vocabulary: talk about what you do in your free time
- Grammar: use *gustar* + verb
- Skills: recognise and learn patterns in radical-changing verbs

Mira el video. ¿Qué deportes y pasatiempos se mencionan?

Watch the video and note down the sports and hobbies mentioned.

Ejemplo: yachting, golf ...

 **Gramática →** p.167

Gustar

You have already met *gustar* used with a noun; look back at page 40.

For example: *Me gusta la música y me gustan los conciertos de música pop.*

Now you can use it with a verb as follows:

Me gusta escuchar música y tocar la trompeta.

Me gusta	Nos gusta	tocar el piano
Te gusta	Os gusta	ver la tele
Le gusta	Les gusta	salir con amigos

I like to play (playing) the piano, etc.

What is the name for the part of the verb – *tocar* – which follows the phrase *me gusta*?

Escucha e indica el pasatiempo.

Listen and point to the hobby mentioned.

Ejemplo: 1 b

a jugar al ajedrez

b tocar la guitarra

c  ir al cine

d  montar a caballo

e  bailar salsa

f  jugar con videojuegos

Habla con tu compañero.

NC 2–3

Ask your partner which of the activities they like doing.

A ¿Qué te gusta hacer?
B Me gusta bailar salsa.
A La letra e.

Escribe.

NC 2–3

Write about your partner.

Ejemplo: A Grace le gusta bailar salsa.

See Zoom OxBox

5 **Escucha el diálogo.**
Listen to the conversation between Elena and Carlos. Who

1 adores swimming?
2 is bored with television?
3 is interested in cinema?
4 hates computer games?
5 is over the moon about their new iPod?
6 likes surfing the internet?

☺	☹
me gusta	no me gusta
me encanta	me aburre
me apasiona	me molesta
me interesa	me fastidia
me flipa	
me mola	

Gramática → p.166

Here are some more commonly used radical-changing verbs.

poder (ue)	**preferir (ie)**	**querer (ie)**
to be able to	to prefer	to like/want
p**ue**do	pref**ie**ro	qu**ie**ro
p**ue**des	pref**ie**res	qu**ie**res
p**ue**de	pref**ie**re	qu**ie**re
podemos	preferimos	queremos
podéis	preferís	queréis
p**ue**den	pref**ie**ren	qu**ie**ren

Which letter changes and how does it change?
How do these compare to the verb *jugar*?

After completing Activity 6, list all the radical-changing verbs used.

 6 **Lee y contesta a las preguntas.**
Read the 'tweets' below and answer the questions.

1 What does he/she prefer to do when it rains?
2 When do they like playing football?
3 When does he/she prefer to play tennis?
4 What happens when it is stormy?
5 What can the weather be like for athletics?

? Think

Check the spelling of all the sports and hobbies that look like the English equivalent word.
Example: tennis – *el tenis*

Make a note of the difference. Then make a note of how the pronunciation changes.

El tiempo y tus pasatiempos

Si hace sol prefiero jugar al tenis.

Cuando llueve prefiero ir al cine.

Puedo practicar esquí cuando nieva.

No podemos hacer surf si hay tormenta.

Cuando hace mucho sol no nos gusta practicar ciclismo.

Si hay viento puedo hacer windsurf.

Quiero hacer atletismo, no importa si hace frío o calor.

Todos queremos jugar al fútbol en primavera, verano, otoño e invierno, todo el año.

Challenge

List five of your favourite hobbies and sports and give a reason why you like each one.

Example: Me gusta tocar el piano porque me encanta la música clásica. **NC 3–4**

2A.3 Por la mañana

- Vocabulary: say what you do in the morning
- Grammar: use reflexive verbs
- Skills: explain patterns in verbs

06:45
07:00
07:05
07:15
07:25
07:30

Gramática → p.165

Reflexive verbs

You will find these verbs in your dictionary with *se* attached to the end of the verb. Example: *levantarse* – to get up (to get **oneself** up)

These verbs have a reflexive pronoun which normally comes before the verb.

me levanto	nos levantamos
te levantas	os levantáis
se levanta	se levantan

- Look at the example above. Can you work out what each verb means? (I get up, you ...)
- Match the personal pronouns to the correct part of the verb.

nosotros ellos yo ella vosotros él tú ellas

desayuno
me ducho
me lavo los dientes
me levanto
me peino
me pongo (el uniforme)

 LEER 1
Empareja.
Match each of the phrases in the vocabulary box with one of the illustrations showing Lucho's morning routine. What does each one mean?

 ESCUCHAR 2
🎧 **Escucha y anota la hora.**
Listen and make a note of the time for each activity.

Ejemplo: gets up – 6.45

What has Lucho forgotten to do?

See Zoom OxBox

Mira el video.
Watch the video. What does Eva do in the morning?

Escucha a Lucía. ¿Verdad o mentira?
Listen to Lucía. True or false?

Ejemplo: 1 verdad (✓)

1 Lucía wakes up at six on the dot.
2 Lucía does yoga after breakfast.
3 She gets dressed before breakfast.
4 Then she does her flute practice.
5 She goes to drama club after school.
6 She has German lessons with her uncle.

Gramática → p.165

Here are two more reflexive verbs which are also radical-changing:

me despierto – *I wake up*
me visto – *I get dressed*

despertarse	vestirse
me desp**ie**rto	me v**i**sto
te desp**ie**rtas	te v**i**stes
se desp**ie**rta	se v**i**ste
nos despertamos	nos vestimos
os despertáis	os vestís
se desp**ie**rtan	se v**i**sten

What do *nos despertamos, te despiertas, se visten* and *os vestís* mean?

? Think

Almuerzo means 'I have lunch'. Now work out the infinitive form and write down the whole verb.

Copia el texto. Escribe los verbos correctos.
Copy the text and write out the verbs in the first person singular.

Ejemplo: 1 me despierto

En el verano **1** _____ (*despertarse (ie)*) temprano – a las seis normalmente. Durante la semana **2** _____ (*bañarse*) rápidamente y **3** _____ (*ponerse*) el uniforme para ir al instituto.

Siempre **4** _____ (*desayunar*) café con leche y cereales. Al llegar al instituto **5** _____ (*jugar(ue)*) en el patio con mis amigos. A la una **6** _____ (*almorzar(ue)*) en el comedor.

Escribe los verbos en la 3ª persona.
Now write the verbs in Activity 5 in the third person singular.

Challenge
Create a dialogue with a partner about your morning routine.
Ask about times and try to use all the verbs on these two pages.

Example: ¿A qué hora te despiertas?
¿Te levantas a las seis en punto?

NC 3–4

 See Zoom OxBox

- Vocabulary: talk about what you do after school
- Grammar: use the full verb *ir* – to go
- Skills: use sequencing to add interest and cohesion to what you write and say

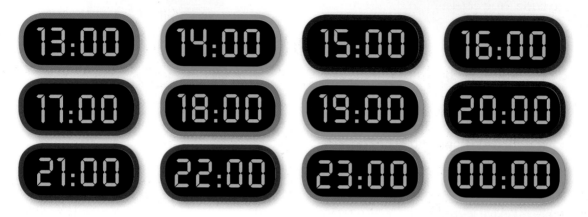

13:00 14:00 15:00 16:00
17:00 18:00 19:00 20:00
21:00 22:00 23:00 00:00

HABLAR 1

Juega.
Play a game with a partner.

A Trece horas.
B Es la una de la tarde.

en punto
a eso de

ESCUCHAR 2

Escucha y contesta a las preguntas.
Listen to Bartolomé talking about his daily routine and answer the questions.

1 What time does school finish?
2 What does Bartolomé do first when he gets home?
3 Then what does he do?
4 What time does he take the dog for a walk?

5 Does he have supper before or after doing his homework?
6 For how long does he watch TV?
7 What time does he go to bed?
8 What time does he fall asleep?

descansar   merendar (ie)   ver la tele   pasear al perro

hacer los deberes   cenar   acostarse (ue)   dormirse (ue)

 **See Zoom OxBox**

3 **Lee los textos. ¿Adónde van Manuela y Rebeca?**
Read the texts. Where do Manuela and Rebeca go?

Ejemplo: Primero Manuela va al centro comercial.

Manuela
Primero voy al centro comercial a hacer compras; luego voy a nadar a la piscina; después voy a casa a cenar con mis padres; más tarde quiero ir al cine con José y Felix; ¡y finalmente voy a casa a dormir!

Rebeca
Pues yo, primero voy a la biblioteca a estudiar; luego mis padres y yo vamos al Museo de Arte Contemporáneo a ver una exposición nueva; por último vamos a cenar en un restaurante peruano.

Gramática → p.166

Irregular verbs
You have already come across the irregular verbs *tener* and *ser* (see page 18).

Can you remember what we mean by the term 'irregular' verb?
Here is another irregular verb you need to learn off by heart.

ir – to go

voy	vamos
vas	vais
va	van

Can you say what each part means in English?

4 **Escucha. ¿Quién habla, Manuela o Rebeca?**
Listen. Who is speaking, Manuela or Rebeca?

? **Think**

Can you guess what each of these sequencing words means? Check in a dictionary or with your teacher. Work with a partner and think of a way to try and remember them. Make up a rap or a game to help you.

primero – *Firstly*
luego – *Then*
entonces – *Then*
después – *After*
más tarde – *Later*
finalmente / por último – *Finally*

5 **Mira el video-blog. ¿Qué contestan Eva, José y Marisa?**
Watch Eva, José and Marisa chatting about sports. Note down their answers to the questions below.

- ¿Qué deporte practicas?
- ¿Qué deporte prefieres?
- ¿Quién es tu deportista preferido?
- ¿Cuál es tu equipo de fútbol preferido?

Challenge

Write a blog about what you do after school. Use the sequencing words and the times of day. Make sure you include some radical-changing verbs as well.

Swap papers with a partner and ask questions about what is written. See how much you can answer from memory.

NC 3–4

See Zoom OxBox

- Vocabulary: talk about weekend activities; recognise and use additional vocabulary on sports and hobbies

Los sábados

Escucha y anota. ¿Qué les gusta hacer los sábados y qué no les gusta hacer?

Listen and make notes. What do they like and dislike doing on Saturdays?

Ejemplo: 1 ☺ *sleeping until 10 /* ☹ *getting up early*

HABLAR 2

NC 2–3

Habla con tu compañero. Da tres respuestas para cada pregunta.

Talk to your partner, giving three answers for each question.

- ¿Qué te gusta hacer los sábados?
- ¿Qué te flipa?
- ¿Qué te fastidia de los sábados?
- ¿Qué odias?

LEER 3

Copia y completa el texto con los verbos correctos de la casilla.

Copy and complete the text with the correct verbs from the box.

> puedo tenemos vamos
> es me acuesto desayuno
> soy encanta jugar me baño

Hoy ▒▒▒ sábado y me ▒▒▒ porque ▒▒▒ levantarme tarde a eso de las diez y media. ¡Qué guay! Primero voy a la cocina donde ▒▒▒ tostadas con mermelada y mis cereales favoritos. Después ▒▒▒ y voy al polideportivo porque ▒▒▒ miembro del equipo de baloncesto. Me gusta ▒▒▒ toda la mañana. Por la tarde ▒▒▒ a Vilanova porque ▒▒▒ un partido contra El Instituto Pío Baroja. Normalmente ▒▒▒ tarde los sábados por la noche.

See Zoom OxBox

Los domingos

LEER 4

Lee el diario de Eva y contesta a las preguntas.
Read Eva's diary and answer the questions.

---

junio
domingo 20

Hoy domingo, es el cumpleaños de mi abuela. Vamos con toda la familia a Sitges a comer en un restaurante que se llama La Santa María. Vamos en tren porque es más fácil ¡y mis padres dicen que pueden beber y comer sin problemas!

Normalmente en el verano hace buen tiempo y podemos comer en la terraza frente al mar; pero claro, si llueve, hay un comedor en el interior.

Mi abuela se llama Clarisa y tiene ochenta y dos años bien cumplidos. Todavía es una persona muy activa. Me encanta su carácter porque es muy cariñosa y adora a todos sus nietos.

Todos nos vestimos con ropa elegante. Yo, por ejemplo, me pongo un traje de flores y no los vaqueros de todos los días. Me mola salir con mi familia y siempre lo pasamos bomba.

? Think

Try to get used to analysing a text to make sense of what is written. In this case, try to find the following:

- five different verbs. Translate them, say what person they are, and what type of verb.
- five adjectives, and comment on their endings.
- two expressions of weather
- two expressions of preference

1 Why is Eva going to Sitges?
2 Why are the family going by train?
3 What's the weather like as a rule?
4 What happens if it rains?
5 What three things does Eva mention about her grandmother?
6 What comment does she make about what she is going to wear?
7 Do you think she enjoys the outing? Why?

Challenge

Write a blog about what you like to do best on a Sunday or on family occasions. Give reasons and try to describe in detail what you do.

NC 3–4

▶ **See Zoom OxBox**

Comprender – Verbs

A Radical-changing verbs

These verbs change their spelling in the root or stem of the verb. Can you work out why this part of the verb is called the root or the stem?

u → ue
o → ue
e → ie

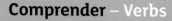

jugar	poder	preferir	querer
juego	puedo	prefiero	quiero
juegas	puedes	prefieres	quieres
juega	puede	prefiere	quiere
jugamos	podemos	preferimos	queremos
jugáis	podéis	preferís	queréis
juegan	pueden	prefieren	quieren

Think about the pattern. Where do the changes **not** happen?

1 Copy the sentence and choose the correct form of the verb.

1 Juan qu_____ jugar al baloncesto esta tarde.

2 Ellos pref_____ ir al cine.

3 Hoy mi amigo no p_____ salir.

4 Nosotros j_____ al fútbol todos los lunes.

5 ¿Qué día j_____ vosotros?

B Reflexive verbs

These verbs have a (reflexive) pronoun in front of them. It changes to match the subject (the person or thing 'doing' the verb).

Can you remember how these verbs are presented in a dictionary? Check pages 57 and 59.

me levanto	nos levantamos
te levantas	os levantáis
se levanta	se levantan

Why do you think they are called reflexive verbs? (Clue = 'self'.)

Put *no* in front of the pronoun if you want to make the sentence negative.

no me despierto   no te despiertas

Continue and write out the verb in full.

2 Use reflexive verbs to say the following in Spanish.

1 We wake up at six thirty.
2 They get up at a quarter to seven.
3 I take a shower first.

4 Then I get dressed.
5 They go to bed at ten thirty.
6 They fall asleep at about 11 o' clock.

See Zoom OxBox

Aprender – Learning verbs

C Pronouns and verb patterns

Remember that verbs in Spanish don't need the personal pronoun in front of them for you to recognise who is doing the action.

3 Can you write down the personal pronouns in sequence (from *yo*, I)?

> yo él nosotros
> vosotros usted ellos
> ellas ustedes ella tú

Recognise the pattern sequence for regular verbs:

AR = O AS A AMOS ÁIS AN

4 Now write out the sequence for regular verbs ending in *-er* and *-ir*.

5 Now do the same for *ser* and *tener*.

Make up a jingle or a rap, or sing the endings to your favourite tune to make sure you learn them.

Write **irregular** verbs onto cards – Spanish on one side and English on the other.

What else do you have to remember about the verb *tener*?
Can you think of more ways to help you learn verbs?

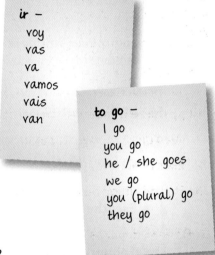

> ir –
>   voy
>   vas
>   va
>   vamos
>   vais
>   van

> to go –
>   I go
>   you go
>   he / she goes
>   we go
>   you (plural) go
>   they go

6 Find the Spanish sequencing words that go with these English ones.

> last   later   next   first   then   afterwards

Why do you think it is helpful to use words like this when you speak or write?

Hablar – Pronunciation

D The sounds of the letters j and g

7 Listen and repeat these sounds.

ja – je – ji – jo – ju

Javier   Jerónimo   Jiménez   Jorge   Julio

Think about how you have produced this sound.
Which part of your mouth does the sound come from?

Now do the same for these words.

gato gorila gusano gerbo gigante

Which words sound like the **j** words?

Which would you call hard-sounding words and which soft-sounding?

Learn this sentence by heart.
La tortuga gigante juega con la guapa jirafa al ajedrez.

See Zoom OxBox

- Vocabulary: revise sports and hobbies
- Grammar: practise using radical-changing verbs
- Skills: follow an example to begin to write independently

ESCUCHAR 1 NC 2

🎧 **Escucha e identifica el deporte.**
Listen and identify each sport.

Ejemplo: **1** *football = c*

ESCUCHAR 2

🎧 **¿Qué deporte no se menciona?**
Which sport isn't mentioned?

LEER 3 NC 3

Completa el diálogo con el verbo adecuado.
Complete the conversation with the appropriate verbs.

> **Manuela:** Me encanta **(a)** _____ salsa pero no me gusta **(b)** _____ la tele.
>
> **Alejandro:** Pues a mí me fascina **(c)** _____ la trompeta y también me apasiona **(d)** _____ música.
>
> **Manuela:** Bueno, a mí me aburre **(e)** _____ libros y me molesta mucho **(f)** _____ al fútbol.
>
> **Alejandro:** Vale, pero entonces ¿qué te interesa **(g)** _____ en tu tiempo libre?

> **Remember!**
> jugar a + el fútbol = jugar **al** fútbol

> hacer jugar tocar escuchar
> bailar ver leer

ESCUCHAR 4

🎧 **Escucha y verifica.**

LEER 5 NC 2–3

Lee el anuncio. ¿Quién es? Identifica a la persona.

Read the advert and identify who the writer is.

> Hola, tengo 12 años y quiero tener amigos de todas las partes del mundo. Me gusta leer y veo mucha tele. Me flipa la música grunge y me apasiona tocar la batería y el saxofón. Me fastidia mucho hacer deporte y no me gustan los videojuegos – son aburridos.

HABLAR 6 NC 2–3

👥 **Juega: Adivina quién soy.**
Play 'Guess who I am'.

A ¿Te gusta dibujar?
B ¿Te llamas Pepe?
A ¿Te llamas Luisa?

B No, pero me gusta leer.
A No, no me llamo Pepe.
B Sí, así es.

ESCRIBIR 7 NC 2–3

Escribe un anuncio similar para ti.
Write similar sentences to the ones in the text in Activity 5.

See Zoom OxBox

2A.7 / Extra Plus

- Vocabulary: revise sports and hobbies in a wider context
- Skills: prepare a dialogue; write independently

  Escucha. ¿Verdad (✓) o mentira (✗)?

NC 2–3 *Ejemplo: I like playing football on Mondays. [✓]*

1 I like playing basketball on Thursdays.
2 I am bored with playing golf on Tuesdays.
3 I'm fed up with boxing every Friday.
4 I love cycling on Tuesdays.
5 I don't like doing athletics on Mondays.

  Escucha otra vez.

1 What do they do on Saturdays and Sundays?
2 What is their opinion?

  Lee la entrevista. Empareja las respuestas con las preguntas.

NC 2
1 ¿Quién es tu deportista preferido/a?
2 ¿Qué deporte practica?
3 ¿Cómo es (físicamente)?
4 ¿Cuál es tu equipo preferido?
5 ¿Qué colores tiene?
6 ¿Qué deporte prefieres tú?

a Juega al fútbol.
b Prefiero el Barça.
c Me encanta el surf.
d Se llama Lionel Messi.
e Rojo y azulgrana.
f Tiene el pelo largo y liso – es guapo.

  Escucha y verifica.

  Haz un diálogo usando las preguntas 1–6 de la Actividad 3.

NC 3

  Lee la ficha. Contesta a las preguntas.

NC 3

Apellido: NADAL	**Familia:** una hermana
Nombre: Rafael	**Deporte:** tenis
Fecha de nacimiento: 03-06-1986	**Otro:** pesa 85 kg; mide 185 cm; zurdo
Lugar de nacimiento: Manacor – Mallorca	(usa la mano izquierda); pelo negro y liso;
Nacionalidad: español	su apodo es el torito español

1 ¿Cómo se llama?   3 ¿Tiene hermanos?   5 ¿Cómo es?
2 ¿Cuántos años tiene?   4 ¿Qué deporte practica?

Rellena una ficha para tu deportista preferido/a.

NC 4

 See Zoom OxBox

Escuchar
Listen and say whether it's Sergio or Lorena.

Example: **1** Lorena

Who ...
1 goes swimming on Sunday mornings?
2 enjoys going to museums?
3 loves reading magazines?
4 hates playing football in the rain?
5 does sport in the summer?
6 plays the drums in a band?

Hablar
Complete these sentences to speak about yourself.

1 Durante el otoño ...   4 Hoy hace ... y ...
2 Me fascina ...   5 No me gusta ... pero sí ...
3 Me aburre ...

Leer
Read the text and spot six differences in the picture.

¡Hola! ¿Qué tal? Hoy martes 13 es mi cumpleaños – tengo 13 años. Mi deportista preferido se llama Cesc Fàbregas pero no me gusta mucho su equipo, el Arsenal; prefiero el Real Madrid – los Galácticos que visten de blanco. Me apasiona montar a caballo porque puedo practicarlo todo el año, en invierno cuando hace frío y en verano cuando hace calor. También me mola tocar la trompeta con un grupo de amigos; nos llamamos los Bravos de Barcelona.

Escribir
Write the weather report.

See Zoom OxBox

Vocabulario

El tiempo	The weather
hace buen tiempo	it's fine / it's a nice day
hace mal tiempo	it's bad weather / it's not a nice day
hace sol	it's sunny
hace calor	it's hot
hace frío	it's cold
hace viento	it's windy
hay tormenta	it's stormy
hay niebla	it's foggy
hay nubes	it's cloudy
llueve	it's raining
nieva	it's snowing
la primavera	spring
el verano	summer
el otoño	autumn
el invierno	winter
jugar a / al / a la	to play
el fútbol	football
el baloncesto	basketball
el ciclismo	cycling
el atletismo	athletics
el boxeo	boxing
la pelota vasca	pelota
el voleibol	volleyball

Tiempo libre	Free time
ver la tele	to watch TV
salir con amigos	to go out with friends
tocar la guitarra	to play the guitar
ir al cine	to go to the cinema
montar a caballo	to ride a horse
bailar en la disco	to dance in a disco
jugar al ajedrez	to play chess
jugar con videojuegos	to play computer games
me apasiona	I love
me aburre	it's boring
me molesta	it annoys me
me fastidia	it gets on my nerves
navegar por internet	to surf the net
poder	to be able
preferir	to prefer
prefiero	I prefer
querer	to like / want
si	if
sí	yes

Por la mañana	In the morning
levantarse	to get up
lavarse	to get washed
me lavo (los dientes)	I clean (my teeth)
ducharse	to have a shower
cepillarse	to brush

me cepillo (el pelo)	I brush my hair
peinarse	to comb / do hair
ponerse	to put on (clothes)
desayunar	to have breakfast
despertarse	to wake up
vestirse	to dress
almorzar (ue)	to have lunch

Por la tarde	In the afternoon
a las trece horas	at 13:00 hours (1 p.m.)
descansar	to relax
merendar (ie)	to have a snack
pasear al perro	to walk the dog
hacer los deberes	to do homework
cenar	to have supper
acostarse (ue)	to go to bed
dormirse (ue)	to fall asleep
ir	to go
hacer compras	to do the shopping
la piscina	swimming pool
nadar	to swim

El fin de semana	(At) the weekend
hasta las diez	until ten o' clock
tarde	late
temprano	early
de acuerdo	agreed
montar en bicicleta	to ride a bike
el sábado	on Saturday
los sábados	on Saturdays
la cocina	kitchen
las tostadas	toast
los cereales	cereal
en tren	by train
frente a	opposite
el mar	the sea
pasarlo bomba	to have a great time

I can ...

- talk about the weather
- say what I like and don't like doing (sports and hobbies)
- say what I do in the morning, afternoon and at weekends
- use the radical-changing verbs *jugar*, *poder*, *preferir* and *querer*
- use reflexive verbs
- use sequencing words
- understand idiomatic set phrases, such as using *hacer* to talk about the weather

See Zoom OxBox

- Vocabulary: say where you live
- Grammar: differentiate between *ser* and *estar*
- Skills: pronounce cognates correctly

a la montaña

b la costa

c el campo

d la ciudad

e un pueblo

f una aldea

 ESCUCHAR **1**

🎧 **Escucha y empareja.**
Listen and match the speakers to the pictures.
Draw an arrow for the cardinal point mentioned.

Ejemplo: **1** e ←

 LEER **2**

¿Qué significan las palabras subrayadas?
What do the underlined words mean?

BARRIOS de MADRID

Vivo en <u>el barrio</u> del Retiro, <u>es</u> muy bonito. <u>Está</u> en el centro de la ciudad.

Vivo en el barrio de Villaverde. <u>Está</u> a <u>las afueras</u>, al sur de la ciudad. <u>Es</u> bastante tranquilo.

No vivo en Madrid, vivo en un pueblo al norte de la ciudad. <u>Está</u> cerca del barrio de Fuencarral pero <u>lejos del</u> centro y <u>es</u> histórico.

 See Zoom OxBox

Gramática → p.166

Note how *es* and *está* are used in Activity 2.

In Spanish *ser* and *estar* both mean 'to be': use *ser* to describe something or someone and *estar* to refer to location.

¿Es or *está*?

- Madrid   en España.
- El Parque del Retiro   muy bonito.
- Barcelona   una ciudad bastante grande.
- Andalucía   al sur del país.

Think

Remember to sound Spanish when you pronounce words that are similar to English. Pronounce every letter in the word except the 'h' which is silent.

Pronouncing the vowel sounds correctly is particularly important with cognates:

a [ah] like <u>a</u>nt, e [eh] like <u>e</u>nergy, i [ee] like <u>i</u>nnocent, o [oh] like <u>O</u>bama, u [oo] like b<u>oo</u>t

ESCUCHAR 3 🎧 **Escucha y repite.**
Listen and repeat these places in town.

LEER 4 **Lee. ¿Verdad, mentira o no se menciona?**
Read what Javier says. True, false or not mentioned?

1 Melipilla es la capital de Chile.
2 Javier vive en una aldea al norte de la capital.
3 En Melipilla hay una universidad.
4 A Javier le gusta donde vive.
5 La catedral de Melipilla es muy bonita.

> Vivo en la ciudad de Melipilla al norte de la capital, en Chile. Vivo en el centro donde hay mucho tráfico pero me gusta porque hay muchos sitios que visitar y donde pasar el tiempo. En la ciudad hay un zoo, dos cines, dos hospitales, varias discotecas y muchos supermercados pero no hay catedral.

Could you have worked out the meaning of these words even without a picture? With a good dose of common sense language learning is a lot easier!

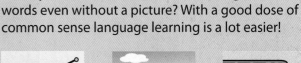

un supermercado   un parque   una estación

un restaurante   una catedral   una discoteca
un banco   un instituto   un cine
un museo

HABLAR 5 **Habla. ¿Qué hay en tu barrio? ¡Practica!**
What is there where you live?
NC 2

	En mi barrio hay ...	pero no hay ...
1		
2		
3		

Challenge

Copy the letter and replace the pictures with words.

Vivo en Bolivia en una ciudad que se llama La Paz. Vivo cerca del centro de la ciudad al **N** del país. Mi barrio está cerca de la 🏛 de Nuestra Sra. de la Paz. En mi ciudad hay dos 🎦, un 🛒 y muchos 🍽. También hay un 🏛 y una 🚆 pero no hay 🏥. Me ❤❤❤ mi barrio porque es muy turístico.

Now write a passage about where you live. **NC 3–4**

2B.2 ¿Dónde está?

- Vocabulary: give and understand directions
- Grammar: use simple imperatives
- Skills: extend sentences using frequency adverbs

a el parque de atracciones

b la bolera

c el polideportivo

d la piscina

e la oficina de Correos

f el ayuntamiento

g la iglesia

h los grandes almacenes

i la parada de autobús

j las tiendas

ESCUCHAR 1

¿Adónde va Javier? Escucha y rellena la tabla en inglés.
Where does Javier go? Listen and fill in the table in English.

Where?	How often?
1d swimming pool	three times a week

ESCRIBIR 2
NC 3

Escribe. ¿Adónde vas?
Write a few sentences. Where do you go?

Ejemplo: Voy al instituto todos los días pero ...

Gramática → p.163

Voy a ...	→	I go/am going to ...
a + el = al		Voy **al** instituto.
a + la = a la		Voy **a la** piscina.

siempre
todos los días
a menudo
a veces
nunca
una vez a la semana
dos veces a la semana
de vez en cuando

? Think

To reach a higher level, get into the habit of extending your sentences using connectives (*pero, sin embargo, también* etc.) and using opinions (*me gusta, no me gusta* etc.).

See Zoom OxBox

ESCUCHAR 3

🎧 **Escucha. ¿En qué orden se mencionan?**

Listen. In which order are these phrases mentioned?
Where do the people want to go?

*Ejemplo: **1** e, piscina*

a Sigue todo recto

b Tuerce a la izquierda

c Tuerce a la derecha

d Cruza el puente

e Cruza la calle

f Toma la primera calle a la izquierda

g Toma la primera calle a la derecha

h Toma la segunda calle a la izquierda

i Toma la tercera calle a la derecha

Está aquí

? Think

There are several ways of asking for directions. What is the simplest way?

⚙ Gramática → p.166

Remember that in Spanish we have familiar and polite forms. If you are giving instructions ...

to a friend:	to an older person:
Sigue	Siga
Tuerce	Tuerza
Cruza	Cruce
Toma	Tome

 LEER 4

Lee las frases. ¿Adónde van?

Read the sentences. Where are the people going?

*Ejemplo: **1** estación*

1 Sigue todo recto, toma la tercera calle a la izquierda y está a mano derecha.

2 Tuerce a la derecha, cruza el puente y está a mano izquierda.

3 Toma la tercera calle a la izquierda, sigue todo recto y está en frente.

4 Toma la primera calle a la izquierda, sigue todo recto, cruza la calle y está a la izquierda.

 HABLAR 5

NC 2–3

👥 **Hablar. ¿Cómo se va a ...?**

With a partner, take it in turns to ask and answer how to get to the different places in town. Use the map in Activity 4.

 **Challenge**

Write directions to get from your school to a nearby place your classmates and teachers will know. Read them out loud and see who can work out where they are going. NC 2–3

 **See Zoom OxBox**

2B.3 Mi casa

- Vocabulary: name the rooms in a house
- Grammar: use prepositions correctly
- Skills: improve your speaking and writing using adjectives

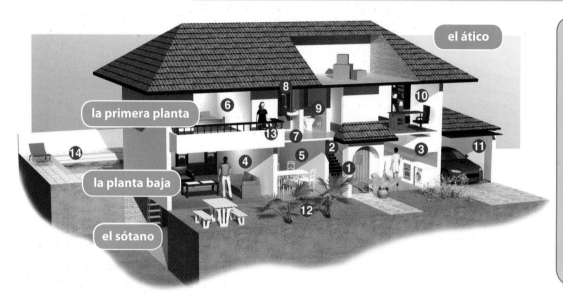

el ático

la primera planta

la planta baja

el sótano

1	una entrada
2	unas escaleras
3	una cocina
4	un salón
5	un comedor
6	un dormitorio
7	un cuarto de baño
8	una ducha
9	un aseo
10	un despacho
11	un garaje
12	un jardín
13	un balcón
14	una piscina

VIDEO 1

Mira el video. ¿Qué dice Marisa de su casa?
Watch the video. What does Marisa say about her house?
Which rooms does she mention?

LEER 2

NC 2

Copia y completa.
Copy the text, replacing the pictures with the words for the appropriate rooms.

*Ejemplo: En casa tenemos un **sótano** muy oscuro ...*

En casa tenemos un ☗ muy oscuro donde mi padre tiene su vino. En la planta baja hay un 🚗 enorme, una 🥘 bastante moderna y grandísima y un 🛋 muy acogedor, pero no tenemos 🍴. También hay un 🚽 nuevo. En la primera planta hay dos 🛏🛏. El 🛏 de mis padres es azul y el mío es de color rosa. Además hay un 🛏 antiguo pero limpio y un 💻 pequeño. Mi casa no tiene △ pero tiene un 🏠 bastante espacioso. Fuera hay un 🌱 muy bonito.

ESCUCHAR 3

Escucha y verifica.
Listen and check your answers.

LEER 4

Identifica los 13 adjetivos de la Actividad 2.
Find the 13 adjectives in Activity 2. Look up their meaning in the dictionary if you don't already know them.

? Think

How have the adjectives been enhanced in Activity 2? Remember to enhance your adjectives to improve your own speaking and writing.

See Zoom OxBox

Don Quijote está <u>enfrente de</u> Sancho.

Sancho está <u>detrás de</u> Don Quijote.

Sancho está <u>al lado de</u> Don Quijote. Don Quijote está <u>a la izquierda de</u> Sancho. Sancho está <u>a la derecha</u> de Don Quijote.

Dulcinea está <u>entre</u> Don Quijote y Sancho.

LEER 5

NC 3–4

Escribe las habitaciones en el plano.
Read the description and label the floor plans.

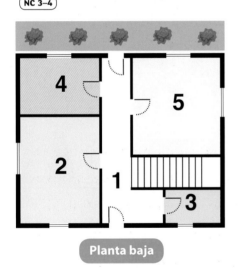

Planta baja

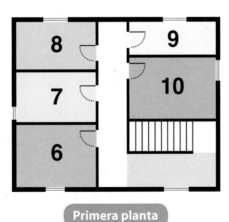

Primera planta

En la planta baja está la entrada. A la izquierda de la entrada hay un salón y enfrente del salón hay un aseo con unas escaleras al lado. Al lado del salón está la cocina y enfrente de la cocina está el comedor. Detrás de la casa hay un jardín.

En la primera planta hay tres habitaciones. Enfrente de las escaleras hay un cuarto de baño. A la derecha del cuarto de baño está el dormitorio de mis padres y al lado está mi dormitorio. El dormitorio de mi hermano está entre las escaleras y un despacho.

? Think

Did you know that Don Quijote and Sancho Panza are the most important characters in Spanish literature?

? Think

Did you notice how to say 'my parents' bedroom' and 'my brother's bedroom'?

How would you say ...
• my dad's office?
• my sister's friend?
• my friend's cat?

una granja	una casa
un chalet	un piso
un bloque de pisos	

Challenge

👥 Prepare a detailed description of where you live and the floor plan. Describe it to a partner who will make notes and draw the plan. Do the same for them. NC 3–4

 *See Zoom OxBox*

- Vocabulary: say what furniture is in your bedroom
- Grammar: use more prepositions
- Skills: work out the gender of new words

Un dormitorio juvenil

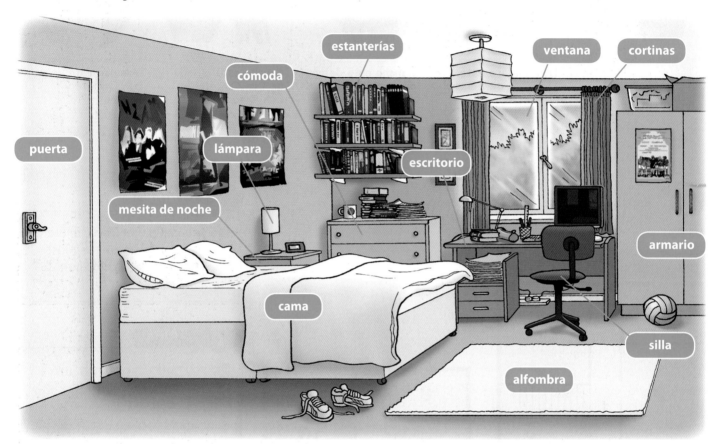

estanterías

cómoda

ventana cortinas

puerta

lámpara

escritorio

mesita de noche

armario

cama

silla

alfombra

 1 ESCRIBIR

NC 2

¿Qué hay en el dormitorio? Descríbelo.
What's in the bedroom?
Write a description, adding *un/una/unos/unas* as appropriate.

Ejemplo: En el dormitorio hay una cama, un ...

 2 ESCRIBIR

NC 3

Mejora la descripción y da tu opinión.
Enhance your description using adjectives (including colours) and quantifiers. Give your opinion of the bedroom.

> grande   pequeño   bonito   moderno   cómodo
> simple   elegante

? **Think**

Are the items in the bedroom masculine or feminine? Singular or plural? Remember that determiners (*el/la/los/las* or *un/una/unos/unas*) and describing words (*blanco, bonito* etc.) agree with the noun.

demasiado
muy
bastante
un poco

 **See Zoom OxBox**

ESCUCHAR 3

¿Dónde está Don Quijote? Escucha y corrige los errores.
Where is Don Quijote? Listen and correct the mistakes.

*Ejemplo: 1 Don Quijote está **dentro del** armario.*

HABLAR 4

NC 3–4

Hablar. Tres en raya.
Speaking: take it in turns with a partner. You only have twenty seconds per turn. Whoever gets three in a row wins.

LEER 5

NC 3–4

Lee la descripción y dibuja el plano.
Read the description and draw a plan of Soraya's bedroom.

Querida amiga,
Mi dormitorio en la casa nueva es bastante grande. El armario está al lado de la puerta y a su izquierda hay una estantería y una mesita de noche. Bueno, hay dos mesitas de noche y la cama está entre las dos. La ventana está enfrente de la puerta y de momento no tiene cortinas. Debajo de la ventana está mi escritorio y delante de éste hay una silla. Al lado del escritorio hay una cómoda y tengo una alfombra super grande entre la cama y la cómoda. ¡Ah! Y tengo dos lámparas, una encima de la mesita cerca de la ventana y la otra encima del escritorio.
¿Cómo es tu dormitorio? Escríbeme pronto.
Soraya

ESCUCHAR 6

Mira el video-blog. Toma notas en inglés.
Watch the young people and make notes in English about their house, bedroom and opinions. How do they answer the following questions?

- ¿Vives en una casa o en un piso?
- ¿Cómo es tu piso?
- Describe tu dormitorio.

Challenge
Write a detailed description of your bedroom.

NC 4

See Zoom OxBox

- Skills: give your opinion about the region where you live

Escoge un adjetivo para cada foto.
Choose an adjective for each picture.

a animado	**d** turístico	**g** industrial
b pintoresco	**e** ruidoso	**h** residencial
c histórico	**f** agrícola	

See Zoom OxBox

2 Lee y elige un adjetivo para cada frase.

NC 3

Read and choose an adjective from Activity 1 for each sentence.

Ejemplo: 1 c

1 Hay muchos monumentos, por ejemplo un anfiteatro, un acueducto, estatuas y museos.

2 No hay ni bares, ni restaurantes ni tiendas. Es una zona tranquila donde viven muchas familias con niños.

3 Es una región muy verde y hay muchas granjas por la zona.

4 Es un lugar muy bonito, con un paisaje muy colorido e interesante.

5 Hay muchos sitios famosos para visitar así que siempre está lleno de extranjeros sacando fotos.

6 Siempre hay mucho ruido por culpa de los constructores, y el tráfico. Nunca hay silencio en esta zona de la ciudad.

7 Hay mucha contaminación por el humo de las fábricas pero también hay mucho empleo.

8 Hay muchos bares y restaurantes y cuando hace calor las calles están llenas de gente paseando o tomando unas tapas en las cafeterías.

3 🎧 Escucha. ¿En qué orden se mencionan los adjetivos de la Actividad 1?

Listen. In which order are the adjectives in Activity 1 mentioned?

4 Lee. ¿Cómo se dice en español?

Read the text about Marisa and find out how to say these words and phrases in Spanish.

1 flat screen television
2 carpet
3 in a corner
4 bunk beds
5 the walls
6 light pink
7 printer
8 laptop
9 speakers

> Voy a contaros cómo es mi dormitorio. Mi dormitorio es más grande que el dormitorio de Khalid. Las paredes están pintadas de un rosa claro y están llenas de pósters de David Bisbal, Robert Pattison y Zac Efron. Tengo tres armarios aunque están llenos de libros. En el suelo hay una moqueta de color violeta pero no tengo alfombras. En mi dormitorio hay literas y a veces se queda una amiga a dormir. Tengo un escritorio en una esquina donde también hay un ordenador viejo y una impresora, aunque también tengo un portátil moderno. Encima de la cómoda tengo un televisor de pantalla plana y un altavoz para mi iPod. El dormitorio tiene dos ventanas grandes con unas cortinas blancas. Me encanta mi dormitorio porque es espacioso y muy femenino.

Challenge

Speaking. Prepare a short presentation about where you live. Ensure you mention all the following points.

- the location of where you live
- what your area/neighbourhood is like
- what your house is like
- the rooms in your house
- what your bedroom is like
- whether you like your bedroom and why (not)

NC 4

ochenta y uno **81**

Comprender – More numbers and verbs

A Ordinal numbers

1st	primero/a	6th	sexto/a
2nd	segundo/a	7th	séptimo/a
3rd	tercero/a	8th	octavo/a
4th	cuarto/a	9th	noveno/a
5th	quinto/a	10th	décimo/a

Beyond 10th, cardinal numbers are generally used:

el octavo piso – *the 8th floor*

el piso catorce – *the 14th floor*

Cardinal numbers are adjectives and so they need to agree in gender and number with what they describe. However, they generally go in front of the noun they describe:

los primero**s** mes**es** – *the first months*

la primer**a** planta – *the 1st floor*

B *Ser* and *estar*

Both *ser* and *estar* have the same meaning: **to be**.

Ser is known as the **permanent** 'to be' and it is used for:
- Origin: **Soy** *de Cuba*, **soy** *cubano*.
- Expressions of time: **Son** *las seis y cuarto.* / *Hoy* **es** *viernes*.
- Occupation: **Mi** *padre* **es** *profesor*.
- Relationships: *Luís y Juan* **son** *mis hermanos*.
- Description: *La casa* **es** *grande*.
- What things are made of: *El barco* **es** *de papel*.

Estar is known as the **temporary** 'to be' and it is used for:
- Temporary states: *Ana* **está** *enferma* (ill).
- Moods: **Estoy** *deprimido*.
- Location/position: *Londres* **está** *en Inglaterra.* / *El coche* **está** *en el garaje*.

ser	estar
soy	estoy
eres	estás
es	está
somos	estamos
sois	estáis
son	están

1 How would you say the following in Spanish?

1. the 7th book
2. the 4th brother
3. the 6th street
4. the 1st days
5. the 12th door
6. the 2nd pool

2 Choose the correct verb and say why you have made that choice.

Example: 1 es – description

1. La lección es/está difícil.
2. El café es/está frío.
3. Los estudiantes son/están argentinos.
4. Susana es/está muy inteligente.
5. El móvil es/está encima de la mesa.
6. El plato es/está de plástico.

3 Translate the following sentences.

1. She is from Málaga.
2. The bus is at the bus stop.
3. The house is in the mountains.
4. The village is very pretty.
5. Maria's brother is a student.

Aprender – Sending a letter

C Spanish addresses

Spanish people have two surnames. Women don't change their surname when they get married so when they have children, the children have the first surname of the father followed by the first surname of the mother.

The first number refers to the floor. The 2° is an abbreviation of *segundo,* which is masculine because of *piso.* Be aware that there could be many flights of stairs to the second floor as you may have a *planta baja* (ground floor) and an *entresuelo* (mezzanine level) before the first floor itself.

C/ is the abbreviation for *Calle* (street). There are many other abbreviations such as *Av/* (*Avenida,* Avenue) and *Ctra/* (*Carretera,* Road). They go at the beginning followed by the name. The street number comes last.

This is the postcode and it only has numbers, no letters.

Josefa Morales Román
C/ Carmen 17, 2° 1ª
08280 Calaf
(Barcelona)

The second digit refers to the flat number on that landing and it has the ª because it refers to *puerta* which is feminine. If there are four levels with a total of eight flats, flats are not numbered from 1 to 8 but rather 1° 1ª, 1° 2ª, 2° 1ª, 2° 2ª, 3° 1ª etc.

Finally you write the province in brackets at the end. This is similar to writing the county in English addresses.

Calaf is the name of the town.

Hablar – Pronunciation

D Vowel sounds

Pronouncing the Spanish vowels correctly can be a challenge, particularly in words that have more than one vowel in one syllable or words that resemble English words.

Remember, in Spanish:

a [ah] – like **a**lphabet   o [oh] – like **o**ctopus

e [eh] – like **E**llie   u [oo] – like f**oo**tball

i [ee] – like **i**ntelligent

4 🎧 **Practise pronouncing these words.
Then listen and check your pronunciation.**

feo (*ugly*)	euros (*euros*)	tierra (*land/earth*)
curioso (*curious*)	autobús (*bus*)	guía (*guide*)
fuera (*outside*)	autocar (*coach*)	violín (*violin*)
viudo (*widower*)	marea (*tide*)	Europa (*Europe*)
aeropuerto (*airport*)	ídolo (*idol*)	

 **See Zoom OxBox**

• Grammar: practise using prepositions and giving directions

1 Busca la palabra intrusa.

NC 1

Find the odd one out. Explain your choice.

Ejemplo: 1 polideportivo – all the others are rooms in a house

1 dormitorio   salón   polideportivo   aseo
2 grande   pequeño   dormitorio   azul
3 puerta   delante   debajo   encima
4 montaña   bolera   costa   campo
5 cama   cómoda   ventana   armario

2 Completa las frases.

NC 2

Complete the sentences with the correct preposition.

> enfrente   detrás   encima   debajo
> entre   dentro   al lado   a la izquierda
> a la derecha

1 El móvil está ▧▧▧ de la cama.
2 Los pósters están ▧▧▧ de la puerta.
3 El gato está ▧▧▧ del armario.
4 El televisor está ▧▧▧ la cómoda y la silla.
5 Los libros están ▧▧▧ de la cama.
6 La lámpara está ▧▧▧ de las cortinas.

3 ¿Adónde van?

NC 2

Where are they going? Read the sentences and look at the map.

Ejemplo: 1 el instituto

1 Está entre el cine y el parque.
2 Está enfrente del parque de atracciones.
3 Está detrás del banco.
4 Está al lado del ayuntamiento.
5 Está enfrente del zoo.
6 Está entre el río y el cine.

Está aquí ★

4 Elige cuatro lugares del mapa. ¿Cómo se va?

NC 3

Choose four places on the street map and give directions from the red star.

Ejemplo: Para ir a la bolera toma la primera calle a la izquierda y sigue todo recto. Está a mano izquierda, al lado del banco.

See Zoom OxBox

- Grammar: practise giving directions and describing where things are

LEER 1

NC 3–4

Mira el mapa. ¿Adónde van?

Ejemplo: 1 Van al ayuntamiento.

1 Toma la primera calle a la derecha, cruza el puente y sigue todo recto. Está a mano izquierda después de la piscina.
2 Sigue todo recto, toma la segunda calle a la derecha. Cruza el puente y tuerce a la izquierda, está a mano izquierda.
3 Toma la primera calle a la izquierda y después la primera a la derecha. Tuerce a la derecha. Está a mano izquierda antes de llegar al instituto.
4 Toma la tercera calle a la derecha y sigue hasta el final. Está en frente, al final de la calle.
5 Están muy cerca delante del río.

6 Toma la primera calle a la derecha y la segunda a la izquierda. Sigue todo recto hasta el final y tuerce a la izquierda. Está entre el cine y el río.

Está aquí ★

LEER 2

NC 2

Categoriza estas palabras. Escribe un/una/unos/unas.

lugares en la ciudad	viviendas	habitaciones en la casa	muebles del dormitorio

bolera dormitorio silla piso granja
cuarto de baño piscina polideportivo
entrada casa cómoda armario escaleras
tiendas chalet castillo salón cama
grandes almacenes estanterías

HABLAR 3

NC 2

¿Dónde están?

1 el niño
2 el pájaro
3 la tienda
4 el banco
5 el perro
6 el colegio de idiomas
7 el coche
8 los libros

Ejemplo: El niño está delante del cine.

ESCRIBIR 4

NC 3–4

Describe tu dormitorio ideal.

En mi dormitorio ideal hay …
Mi dormitorio ideal tiene/es …

? Think

Beware! Some words have more than one meaning. Look at the picture. Besides 'bank', what else do you think *el banco* may mean?

See Zoom OxBox

Escuchar

NC 3

Escuchar

Where do they live? Choose the correct pictures, give their opinion and say why they like/don't like it.

Ejemplo: 1 c, f, h; likes it a lot, quiet

Hablar

NC 2–3

Hablar

Answer the questions.

1 ¿Para ir al polideportivo, por favor?
2 ¿Cómo se va a la bolera?
3 ¿Para ir al supermercado?
4 ¿Cómo se va a la iglesia?
5 ¿Cómo se va a los grandes almacenes?

Está aquí ★

Leer

NC 3–4

Leer

Read Clara's text and answer the questions.

1 Where is Trujillo?
2 Name three things you can do in the city.
3 In what type of accommodation does Clara live? Give two details.
4 Where can you find the bathroom?
5 What is her opinion of her bedroom? Why?
6 What does she have two of?
7 Where is the chest of drawers located?
8 Where would you find the cat if you visited?

Escribir

Escribir

Write a paragraph about where you live.
Mention:

- where it is
- what it is (house, flat, etc.)
- the rooms there are
- the furniture in your bedroom
- your opinion of your bedroom

Vivimos en Trujillo, una ciudad venezolana situada en las montañas de los Andes. La ciudad es muy histórica y se pueden visitar museos, monumentos y la catedral que es de estilo barroco y romántico. Hay muchos restaurantes donde comer, colegios para los niños y un polideportivo a las afueras de la ciudad. Vivimos en una casa grande cerca del centro. La casa tiene tres plantas y un jardín muy bonito detrás. En la planta baja están la entrada, el comedor, la cocina, el salón y el despacho de papá. En la primera planta hay dos dormitorios bastante espaciosos y el cuarto de baño, y arriba está el ático donde yo tengo mi dormitorio. Me encanta mi dormitorio porque tengo una cama muy grande y hay pósters de mis artistas favoritos por todas partes. En mi dormitorio tengo dos armarios y dos ventanas con cortinas blancas. También hay una cómoda al lado de la puerta y un escritorio a la derecha de la cómoda. ¡Ah! Y el gato, claro ... Listo, mi gato; siempre está debajo de la cama.

 See Zoom OxBox

Vivo en ... | I live in ...

Está en ...	*It is in ...*
la montaña	*the mountains*
la costa	*the coast*
el campo	*the countryside*
la ciudad	*the city*
un pueblo	*a town*
una aldea	*a village*
un barrio	*a neighbourhood*
las afueras	*the outskirts*

¿Dónde está? | Where is it?

siempre	*always*
todos los días	*every day*
a menudo	*often*
a veces	*sometimes*
nunca	*never*
una vez a la semana	*once a week*
dos veces a la semana	*twice a week*
un supermercado	*a supermarket*
un parque	*a park*
una estación	*a station*
un banco	*a bank*
un museo	*a museum*
una catedral	*a cathedral*
un zoo	*a zoo*
un colegio	*a school*
un cine	*a cinema*
un parque de atracciones	*a theme park*
la bolera	*the bowling alley*
el polideportivo	*the sports centre*
la piscina	*the swimming pool*
la oficina de Correos	*the post office*
el ayuntamiento	*the town hall*
la iglesia	*the church*
los grandes almacenes	*the department store*
la parada de autobús	*the bus stop*
las tiendas	*the shops*

Sigue/Siga	*Carry on*
Todo recto	*Straight ahead*
Tuerce/Tuerza	*Turn*
Cruza/Cruce	*Cross*
Toma/Tome	*Take*
el puente	*the bridge*
la primera/segunda/tercera	*the first/second/third*
la calle	*the street*
a la derecha	*on the right*
a la izquierda	*on the left*

Mi casa | My house

un sótano	*a basement*
la planta baja	*the ground floor*
la primera planta	*the first floor*
el ático	*the attic*
una entrada	*an entrance hall*
las escaleras	*the stairs*
una cocina	*a kitchen*
un salón	*a living room*
un comedor	*a dining room*
un dormitorio	*a bedroom*
un cuarto de baño	*a bathroom*
una ducha	*a shower*
un aseo	*a toilet*
un despacho	*an office*
un jardín	*a garden*
un balcón	*a balcony*
una piscina	*a swimming pool*

Mi dormitorio | My bedroom

un armario	*a wardrobe*
una cama	*a bed*
un escritorio	*a desk*
unas estanterías	*a bookcase/some shelves*
una mesita de noche	*a bedside table*
una alfombra	*a rug*
una cómoda	*a chest of drawers*
una silla	*a chair*
unas cortinas	*curtains*
una puerta	*a door*
una ventana	*a window*
una lámpara	*a lamp*

delante de	*in front of*
enfrente de	*facing*
detrás de	*behind*
encima de	*on/on top of*
debajo de	*under*
entre	*between*
al lado de	*next to*
cerca de	*near to*
lejos de	*far from*

⊙ **I can ...**

- ⊙ say where I live
- ⊙ talk about what there is in my town
- ⊙ list the rooms in my house
- ⊙ describe my bedroom
- ⊙ use the verbs *ser* and *estar*

 **See Zoom OxBox**

3A.1 Es la hora de comer

- Vocabulary: talk about what you eat at different mealtimes
- Grammar: use nouns and verbs to talk about mealtimes
- Skills: understand the differences between Spanish and English mealtimes

1

2

3

4

 1 Mira los dibujos.
Look at the pictures and decide what the different meals are.

 2 🎧 Escucha y elige la palabra adecuada.
Listen and match the mealtimes to the pictures.

 3 🎧 Escucha otra vez.
Listen again. How do you say 'at about 5 o'clock'?

 4 👥 Habla con tu compañero.

NC 2–3

Tell your partner what time you eat your meals.
They have to note the time down.

Ejemplo: **A** *Tomo el desayuno a las siete y media.*
B *[writes] 7.30 a.m.*

 5 🎧 Escucha e identifica.
Which mealtime are they talking about?

 6 👥 Escribe.

NC 2–3

Write down what time you have your meals.
Compare notes with someone else.

---

el desayuno
la cena
la comida
la merienda
a eso de

⚙ *Gramática* → p.164

To talk about having a meal you can say:
Tomo el desayuno a las siete **or** *Desayuno a las siete.*
Both mean 'I have breakfast at 7 o'clock', but the second way uses the regular verb ***desayunar*** – to have breakfast.

How would you say 1) I have lunch, 2) he has supper, 3) they have tea (an afternoon snack)?
Use these verbs:
comer
merendar (Careful: *yo meriendo*)
cenar

▶ *See Zoom OxBox*

HABLAR 7

¿El desayuno, la comida, la merienda o la cena?
Which meal would you be most likely to eat the following food for?

Ejemplo: 1 la merienda

el chocolate
el pan de ajo
la carne
las verduras
los cereales
los churros
un bocadillo de queso
un paquete de patatas fritas
un pollo asado
una paella
una pizza

1

un paquete de patatas fritas

2

chocolate con churros

3

una paella

4

un bocadillo de queso

7

un pollo asado

5

carne y verduras

6

una pizza y pan de ajo

8

los cereales

ESCUCHAR 8 🎧 **¿Verdadero o falso?**
Listen and decide if the speakers are telling the truth or not.

Ejemplo: 1 falso

LEER 9 **Lee. Copia y completa.**
Read the description and fill in the blanks.

Normalmente en el desayuno tomo c_____, pero el domingo
tomo c_____ con c_____ en la churrería con mi familia.
A mediodía como c_____ y v_____ en el comedor del instituto
con mis amigos. A eso de las cinco, meriendo un b_____ de
q_____. Ceno con mi familia a las ocho y media o las nueve. Mi
cena preferida es p_____, pero también me gusta p_____ a_____.

? Think

Se come is a very useful way of saying in general, people eat something, e.g. *En España se come paella* – In Spain people eat paella.

How else might you say this in English?

How could you be more specific in Spanish and say 'In Spain **they** eat paella'?

Challenge

Design a poster showing what you eat for different meals and at what time. Add comparisons with what a Spanish person might eat and when. Use pictures from magazines, food packets or internet research.

NC 2–3

El desayuno   los cereales   el zumo de naranja   la mermelada

A las 8 horas

las tostadas

▶ **See Zoom OxBox**

- Vocabulary: talk about food you like and dislike, and say what is healthy
- Grammar: use *más que* and *menos que*
- Skills: give a short presentation in Spanish

1 el atún

2 los mariscos

3 las naranjas

4 el pescado

5 el salmón

6 las verduras

7 las gambas

8 los calamares

9 un melocotón

10 un plátano

11 una ensalada verde

12 una manzana

13 la carne

VIDEO 1 **Mira el video.**

Which of the items above do you see in the video?

Ejemplo: 1 el atún

no soporto	odio
no me importa	me encanta
comer	

VIDEO 2 **Mira el video-blog.**

Watch the video and answer the questions.

- What do they like to eat?
- What don't they like?
- What meal do they talk about?
- Do you think they eat healthily?

HABLAR 3

NC 2–3

Haz un sondeo.

Choose six food items. Ask your classmates *¿Te gustan los mariscos? ¿Te gusta el pescado?* etc. Note down their answers.

See Zoom OxBox

ESCUCHAR 4 🎧 **Escucha. Copia y completa.**
Listen and complete the sentences.

*Ejemplo: 1 El postre contiene mucho **azúcar**.*

1 El postre contiene mucho _____ .
2 El helado es _____ .
3 Los perritos calientes son _____ .
4 Las hamburguesas son muy _____ .
5 Las patatas fritas contienen mucha _____ .
6 Los pasteles no son _____ .
7 Los bombones también contienen demasiado _____ .

? Think

El helado contiene mucho azúcar.
El helado is singular.
What do you need to do to the verb *contener* if you want to say that sweets (*los bombones*) have a lot of sugar in them?

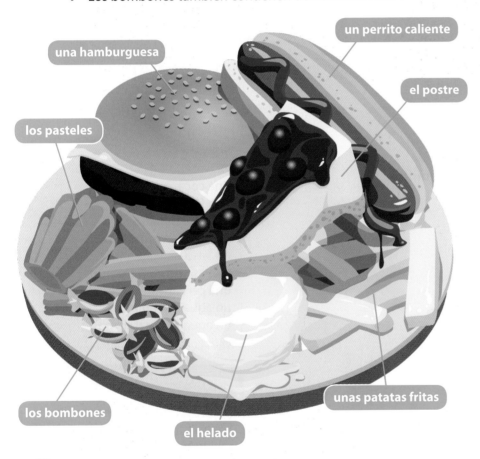

una hamburguesa

un perrito caliente

el postre

los pasteles

los bombones

el helado

unas patatas fritas

contiene mucha grasa
contiene mucho azúcar
es (muy) ...
... sano
... malsano
... soso
... delicioso
son (muy) ...
... sanos/as
... malsanos/as
... sosos/as
... deliciosos/as

⚙️ *Gramática* → p.168

How to say 'more than' and 'less than'

more than – *más que: El pescado es **más** sano **que** los pasteles.*

less than – *menos que: El helado es **menos** sano **que** las verduras.*

ESCRIBIR 5 **Compara la comida.**
Compare the following foods.

NC 2

Ejemplo: 1 Una hamburguesa contiene más grasa que una naranja.

1 hamburguesa – naranja – contiene grasa
2 el pescado – un perrito caliente – sano
3 un melocotón – los bombones – contiene azúcar
4 el postre – una ensalada verde – delicioso
5 las patatas fritas – las gambas – malsano
6 el helado – las verduras – soso

Challenge
Work in a group to give a presentation, with illustrations, about the type of food you and your friends like. The other people in your class will decide how healthy you are. NC 3–4

▶ *See Zoom OxBox*

3A.3 ¡Tengo hambre!

- Vocabulary: ask for food in a café; understand language used when ordering food
- Grammar: use *tengo hambre* and *tengo sed*; use *tú* and *usted*

VIDEO 1 **Mira el video.**

Watch the video. Why does Eva have to hurry home?
What do they decide to drink?

las aceitunas

las patatas

los montaditos

ESCUCHAR 2 **Empareja. Luego escucha e identifica.**

Match the drinks to the words for them.
Then listen and identify them.

Ejemplo: 1 f

a b c d e f g h i

una coca-cola
una fanta naranja
un café solo
un café con leche
un vaso de vino tinto
un vaso de vino blanco
una cerveza
un agua mineral con gas
un agua mineral sin gas

Gramática → p.164

As you found out on page 6, in Spanish there are two ways of saying 'you': *tú* (informal – to your friends and people you know well) and *usted* (formal – to older people, teachers, strangers etc.). The waiter in Activity 2 uses the formal *usted* form of the verb: *¿Qué desea?* – What would you like? and *Aquí tiene* – Here you are. If he were talking to a friend he would say *¿Qué deseas?* and *Aquí tienes*.

HABLAR 3 **Habla con tu compañero.**

Ejemplo: **A** ¿Qué desea?
B Un vaso de vino tinto.
A Aquí tiene.

NC 2

See Zoom OxBox

Escucha y lee.
Listen and read the story. What do they order?

¿Cómo se dice ...?
Find the Spanish in the story above.

Ejemplo: 1 Tengo hambre.

1 I'm hungry.
2 Waiter!
3 Um,
4 For me
5 OK
6 And to eat?
7 for her
8 straight away
9 Here you are.
10 Enjoy your meal.

Escribe una escena. Practica con un compañero.
Write your own café scene. Choose what you would like to eat or drink. Practise it with a partner.

NC 3–4

tengo hambre
tengo sed
para comer
para beber

? **Think**

How else can you use the verb *tener*?
Tengo ... Look back in the book.

Challenge
Using all the food and drink words you have learnt so far design a menu for a café or restaurant.
Invent a conversation like the one in Activity 4. NC 2–4

 See Zoom OxBox

- Vocabulary: invite someone to go out with you, order food and complain
- Grammar: use *ir a*
- Skills: say who you are on the telephone, and complain politely

1 Escucha y lee.

What are Ángel and Rashida talking about?
When, where and at what time do they agree to meet?

Hola, soy Ángel. ¿Está Rashida?

Hola, Ángel, soy yo.
Oye, ¿quieres ir a la cafetería Dalí?

Pues, sí. ¿Cuándo?
Miércoles, por la tarde.

¿A qué hora?
A las siete.

Vale, hasta luego.
Hasta luego.

2 Escucha y escoge.

Listen and choose when, where and at what time the people are meeting.

Ejemplo: 1 c ...

1	Restaurante San Miguel	a	jueves	x	9:00
2	El Bar Marisco	b	sábado	y	2:00
3	Cafetería Lanzarote	c	domingo	z	11:30

? Think

Ángel doesn't say 'Hi, **it's** Ángel', he says *Hola, soy Ángel.*
What does this mean?
How does he ask if Rashida is there?
Rashida doesn't say 'Speaking', she says *Soy yo.* What does this mean?

3 Lee. ¿Adónde van?

Read the text messages. Where are they going and when?

Ejemplo: a Bar Blanco ...

a
¿Quieres ir al Bar Blanco? Jueves a las 5h30 despúes del insti. ¿Vale?

b
Comida de cumpleaños de Lucía, domingo, las 2h, Restaurante de la Playa. ¡Vámonos todos!

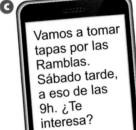
c
Vamos a tomar tapas por las Ramblas. Sábado tarde, a eso de las 9h. ¿Te interesa?

Gramática → p.166

ir a – *to go somewhere*
voy a ... – *I'm going to ...*
vamos a ... – *we're going to*
¿quieres ir a ...? – *do you want to go to ...?*

4 Escribe un mensaje.

NC 3

Write a message to a friend inviting them to a café.

See Zoom OxBox

¡Oiga, camarero!

Lo siento, en seguida.

una cuchara
un tenedor
un cuchillo
¿Dónde está ...?
pedí
hay
una mosca
lo siento
lo traigo
en seguida
traigo otro

Gramática → p.165

Pedí means 'I ordered'. It is a verb in the preterite, a past tense. You will learn more about past tenses later.

a

No tengo cuchara.

b

No tengo cuchillo.

c

No tengo tenedor.

d

¡Hay una mosca en mi café!

e

¡No pedí un bocadillo de jamón, pedí un bocadillo de queso!

f

¿Dónde está mi vino tinto?

ESCUCHAR 5 🎧 **Escucha e identifica el problema.**
Listen and decide what the problem is. Choose from the pictures above.

Ejemplo: 1 c

HABLAR 6 👥 **Habla con tu compañero.**

NC 2
Practise with your partner. One person has a problem, the other identifies it.

Ejemplo: **A** ¡No tengo cuchillo!
         B *b*

Challenge 👥 Prepare and act out a scene in a restaurant or café. Invite your friend by phone, text or email to join you. Order your food and drink. Complain to the waiter. Use the menu you made on page 93. Act out the scene to your class. NC 3–4

 See Zoom OxBox

- Vocabulary: discuss different types of food
- Grammar: practise using adjectives and *se come mucho*
- Skills: be aware of foods in different cultures

Mira el video otra vez.
Watch the beginning of the video again. Eva describes what she had for breakfast – *pa amb tomàquet*. Can you explain what this is?

la comida española   **la comida catalana**   **la comida china**   **la comida india**

la comida rápida   **la comida italiana**   **la comida inglesa**   **la comida vegetariana**   **la comida del instituto**

Escucha. ¿Qué prefieren?
Listen and decide which type of food the people like best.

Ejemplo: 1 la comida china

Habla con tus compañeros. ¿Qué les gusta?
Find three other people who like what you do.

NC 3

Ejemplo: **A** ¿Qué comida te gusta?
       B Me gusta / Prefiero la comida india.

Empareja.
Match the example foods to the food types. Add your own ideas.

NC 2–3

Ejemplo: En la comida china se come mucho arroz.

? Think

What are the different types of food shown here? What helped you work it out?

⚙ Gramática

Remember: *se come mucho …* is a useful way of saying *we / you / they eat a lot of …*

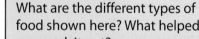

verduras   pescado

patatas   arroz   pasta   patatas fritas   especias   carne

Es muy picante.

Contiene mucha grasa.

Utiliza mucho aceite.

Es muy sosa.

Es muy variada.

Es muy sabrosa.

ESCUCHAR 5

🎧 **Escucha. Copia y completa.**

Listen and complete the descriptions.

*Ejemplo: **1** La comida india es muy picante.*

1 La comida india es ▓▓▓▓
2 La comida china es ▓▓▓▓
3 La comida inglesa ▓▓▓▓ que la comida italiana.
4 La comida vegetariana ▓▓▓▓ carne.
5 La comida rápida ▓▓▓▓ grasa.
6 La comida del instituto es ▓▓▓▓
7 La comida española ▓▓▓▓ pescado.

el arroz
la pasta
las especias
es muy / es poco
contiene mucho
contiene poco
no contiene
utiliza mucho
utiliza poco

HABLAR 6

¿Qué contienen? ¿Se come frío o caliente?

What are they made of? Would you eat them hot or cold?

NC 2–3

Platos típicos de España

la tortilla
la paella
la fabada
el gazpacho

Challenge

Make a poster. Ask different people (friends and/or family members) what types of food they like and why. Find pictures of the types of food and write about them – what do you eat a lot of in that type of food? Is it healthy or unhealthy? What are typical ingredients?

NC 2–4

See Zoom OxBox

Comprender – Comparing two things; using *tú* and *usted*

A Comparing – 'more than' and 'less than'

To make comparisons in English we use 'more than' and 'less than': 'Maths is more difficult than Spanish'. We also add -er to adjectives: 'Spanish is easier than Maths'.

Spanish is easier! You don't need to learn any more word endings. But you still have to remember to check that the verbs and adjectives are correct:

<u>La</u> fruta (f/s) <u>es</u> **más** san<u>a</u> **que** el helado. *Fruit is healthier than ice-cream.*

<u>Las</u> verduras (f/pl) <u>son</u> **más** san<u>as</u> **que** las patatas fritas. *Vegetables are healthier than chips.*

Las verduras contien<u>en</u> **menos** grasa **que** las patatas fritas. *Vegetables contain less fat than chips.*

más sana que ...

1 **Put *más ... que* or *menos ... que* in the correct places in these sentences:**

1 El helado es delicioso las manzanas.
2 El español es difícil la geografía.
3 El profesor de ciencias es simpático la profesora de inglés.
4 Los mariscos son sanos las patatas fritas.

B Using *tú* and *usted*

As you found out on page 6, in Spanish there are four words for 'you'.

Tú and *vosotros* are the familiar ways of saying 'you'. Use them for friends, family and younger people.

Usted and *ustedes* are the polite ways of saying 'you'. Use them to strangers, teachers and older people.

Usted uses the same verb endings as *él* and *ella*. *Ustedes* uses the same verb endings as *ellos* and *ellas*. These are the 3rd person endings.

menos sana que ...

querer – to want		
person	pronoun	verb
1	yo	quiero
2	tú	quieres
3	él / ella / **usted**	quiere
4	nosotros	queremos
5	vosotros	queréis
6	ellos / ellas / **ustedes**	quieren

2 **Which one would you use to:**

1 your headteacher?
2 an elderly couple?
3 your brother?
4 a group of young children?

3 **How would you say:**

1 Hey, Carlos, do you want to go to the café?
2 Do you want a beer, Mr López?

See Zoom OxBox

Aprender – How to remember words

C Grouping words together

Related words

When you come across similar words, write them down together:

el desayuno – breakfast

desayunar – to have breakfast

What other groups of similar words have you seen in this unit?

Groups of expressions

Some verbs can be used with many different expressions.

Record them together:

tener: *tengo hambre* (I'm hungry)

       tengo sed (I'm thirsty)

       tengo doce años (I'm 12 years old)

Add to the list when you come across new examples.

Tomo cerveza ...

D Making up your own examples (memory joggers)

1 Write an example using words you already know with the new word:

   Desayuno *cereales a las siete de la mañana.*

2 Use alliteration – words that begin with the same letter:

   Como **c**arne para la **c**omida.

3 If a verb has changes, write several examples:

   Quiero una coca cola. (yo)

   Queremos una paella. (nosotros)

Write a memory jogger for some words or phrases that you have trouble remembering.

y cereales ...

¡en la cena!

Hablar – Having a conversation

E Talking on the telephone

4 🎧 **Listen to this conversation. Put the sentences in the right order.**

  a ¿A qué hora?

  b Bueno, a eso de las nueve.

  c Adiós.

  d Bien.

  e Diga.

  f El viernes por la tarde.

  g Felipe, soy Ana. ¿Qué tal?

  h Hola, ¿está Felipe?

  i Lo siento, ceno en casa con mi familia.

  j Mm, ¿cuándo?

  k Ohhh, pues, hasta luego Felipe.

  l Oye, ¿quieres ir al bar?

  m Soy yo.

Does Felipe want to go out with Ana? How can you tell? How can this help you when listening to what someone is saying? Why might it not help?

5 🎧 **Listen again. How is this conversation different?**

What do you say when you answer the phone in Spain? This means 'Speak!'

What words do the speakers use to say things like 'well', 'um', 'hey'?

6 👥 **Make up a natural sounding conversation with a partner.**

▶ *See Zoom OxBox*

- Vocabulary: understand problems you might have in a café; identify different meals
- Skills: practise asking for food and drinks in a café

Empareja los dibujos con los problemas.
Match the pictures and the problems.

a No tengo cuchillo.
b ¡Hay una mosca en mi coca-cola!
c No tengo tenedor.

d ¿Dónde está mi bocadillo?
e No tengo cuchara.
f No pedí un café, pedí un vaso de vino.

> un cuchillo
> un tenedor
> una cuchara
> una mosca

Escribe una conversación para cada dibujo.
Write short dialogues to go with these pictures.
Then make up and illustrate some more of your own.

Ejemplo: *Camarero: ¿Qué desea?*
Cliente: Quiero una coca-cola.
Camarero: Aquí tiene.

Lee. ¿Es el desayuno, la comida, la merienda o la cena?
Read and decide which meal it is.

1
- *un agua mineral*
- *un bocadillo de jamón*

2
- *un vaso de vino*
- *una paella*
- *verduras*

3
- *un café con leche*
- *tostadas y mermelada*
- *cereales*

4
- *una fanta naranja*
- *una hamburguesa*
- *una ración de patatas fritas*

See Zoom OxBox

• Skills: solve problems in a café; practise asking for food and drinks in a café; describe different food

 LEER 1

NC 2

Busca una solución para cada problema.

1 No tengo tenedor.

2 No pedí un café solo, pedí un café con leche.

3 ¿Dónde está mi bocadillo?

4 ¡Hay una mosca en mi coca-cola!

a Lo traigo en seguida.

b Lo siento, traigo otra.

 ESCRIBIR 2

NC 3–4

Escribe una conversación en un restaurante.

• The waiter asks you what you want.
• You order a white coffee for you and fizzy orange for your friend.
• The waiter asks if you want anything to eat.
• You want a hamburger and chips, your friend wants some tortilla.
• The waiter says he'll bring it at once.

Make up and write another conversation of your own.
How large a meal can you order?

 ESCRIBIR 3

NC 3–4

Describe las comidas. ¡No digas la verdad!

Ejemplo: Las patatas fritas son muy sanas. El melocotón contiene mucha grasa. El melocotón es menos sano que las patatas fritas.

See Zoom OxBox

Escuchar

NC 2

Listen to the people talking.
What food do they eat for which meal?

Hablar

NC 3–4

How would you order the following items?
How might the waiter reply?

① **②**

Leer

NC 3

Which of the foods described are healthy? Read the article and decide.

La ensalada es una comida muy sana. No contiene mucha grasa. El pescado es más sano que la carne – contiene menos grasa. La fruta – las manzanas o los melocotones – es más sana que los postres. Los postres contienen mucho azúcar. Las hamburgesas y las patatas fritas son muy malsanas, pero en mi opinión, ¡son deliciosas!

burgers	fruit
chips	meat
desserts	salad
fish	

Escribir

NC 3

Describe the foods shown in the pictures. What are they? Do you like them? Are they healthy? Give as much information as you can.

① **②** **③**

See Zoom OxBox

Es la hora de comer	It's time to eat
la cena	evening meal
la comida	midday meal
la merienda	(afternoon) snack
a eso de	at about
el chocolate	chocolate
el pan de ajo	garlic bread
la carne	meat
las verduras	vegetables
los cereales	cereal
los churros	churros
un bocadillo de queso	cheese sandwich
un paquete de patatas fritas	packet of crisps
un pollo asado	roast chicken
una paella	paella
una pizza	pizza

Comida sana	Healthy food
el atún	tuna
los mariscos	shellfish
el pescado	fish
el salmón	salmon
las gambas	prawns
los calamares	squid
un melocotón	peach
un plátano	banana
una ensalada verde	green salad
una manzana	apple
una naranja	orange
contiene mucha grasa	it contains a lot of fat
contiene mucho azúcar	it contains a lot of sugar
es (muy) ...	it's (very)
... sano/a	healthy
... malsano/a	unhealthy
... soso/a	bland
... delicioso/a	delicious
son (muy) ...	they are (very)
... sanos/as	healthy
... malsanos/as	unhealthy
... sosos/as	bland
... deliciosos/as	delicious

¡Tengo hambre!	I'm hungry!
una coca-cola	a coca-cola
una fanta naranja	fizzy orange
un café solo	black coffee
un café con leche	white coffee
un vaso de vino tinto	a glass of red wine
un vaso de vino blanco	a glass of white wine
una cerveza	a beer
un agua mineral con gas	sparkling mineral water
un agua mineral sin gas	still mineral water
tengo hambre	I'm hungry
tengo sed	I'm thirsty
para comer	to eat
para beber	to drink

¡Oiga, camarero!	Waiter!
una cuchara	a spoon
un tenedor	a fork
un cuchillo	a knife
¿Dónde está ...?	Where is ...?
pedí	I asked for
hay	there is
una mosca	a fly
lo siento	I'm sorry
lo traigo	I'll bring it
en seguida	at once
traigo otro	I'll bring another

Me encanta la comida	I love food
el arroz	rice
la pasta	pasta
las especias	spices
es muy / es poco	it's very / it's not very
contiene mucho	it contains a lot (of)
contiene poco	it contains little (not a lot of)
utiliza mucho	it uses a lot (of)
utiliza poco	it uses little (not a lot of)

I can ...

- explain the differences between British and Spanish mealtimes
- talk about healthy and unhealthy food
- say what I like to eat
- order food in a café
- complain in a restaurant
- talk about food in different countries

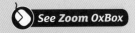

- Vocabulary: talk about means of transport
- Grammar: use the immediate future tense: *voy a viajar*
- Skills: create a dialogue from a model

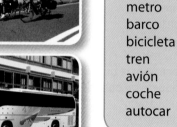

en ...
autobús
metro
barco
bicicleta
tren
avión
coche
autocar

ESCUCHAR 1 🎧 **Escucha y empareja.**
Listen and match the speakers with the forms of transport.

ESCUCHAR 2 🎧 **Escucha y anota los países.**
Listen again and note the order of the countries to be visited.

ESCUCHAR 3 🎧 **¿Qué medios de transporte no se mencionan?**
Which forms of transport are not mentioned?

HABLAR 4 👥 **Practica la conversación.**
Practise the conversation.

NC 2–3

¡Hola! ¿Vas de vacaciones este año?
Creo que sí.
¿Adónde vas?
Voy a España.
¿Cómo vas a viajar?
Voy en tren y después en avión. ¿Y tú, adónde vas?
Pues voy a Italia con mis padres.
¿Cómo vais a viajar?
Vamos en coche porque es más práctico.

es más ...
cómodo   barato
corto   divertido

 Think

Spanish uses the preposition *en*: **en** barco, **en** avión etc.
How do you say the equivalent phrases in English?

HABLAR 5 👥 **Inventa otros diálogos.**
Make up further dialogues of your own.

NC 3

Portugal

Dinamarca

Polonia

Méjico

Estados Unidos

See Zoom OxBox

Gramática → p.166

The immediate future

You use this tense just like you do in English to say what you **are going to do** or what **is going to happen** in the near future.

Take the verb *ir* (to go) + *a* + the **infinitive** of the verb of action:

Voy	a	viajar en tren
Vas	a	visitar Barcelona
Va	a	salir con sus amigos
Vamos	a	volar en avión
Vais	a	comer en un restaurante
Van	a	jugar al tenis.

 Escribe.

NC 3

Write these sentences in Spanish.

1 I am going to play basketball.
2 We are going to eat ice-cream.
3 They are going to live in Argentina.

Make up three more sentences of your own in English. Give them to a partner to write or say in Spanish.

 Mira el video y contesta a las preguntas.

Watch the video and answer the questions.

1 According to Khalid, how much is the train ticket?
2 Which is more expensive – the train or the bus?
3 What does he say about the bus journey?

 Inventa comparaciones ridículas.

NC 2–3

Make up some silly comparisons.

Ejemplo: ¿Es más rápido ir de Barcelona a Madrid a pie o en coche?

 Escucha y repite.

Listen and repeat the conversation.

Buenos días. Un billete de ida y vuelta a Sitges, por favor.

Vale; aquí tiene usted. ¿Algo más?

Sí. ¿A qué hora sale el tren, por favor?

Pues hay trenes cada veinte minutos. Tarda media hora.

Gracias. ¿Cuánto es?

El billete de ida y vuelta cuesta seis euros.

 Inventa otros diálogos.

NC 3–4

Make up more dialogues like the one in Activity 9.

Challenge

Say what form of transport you use to get to school.

Ask a few friends what form of transport they use.

Write a brief paragraph about what form of transport you prefer and why. NC 3–4

- Vocabulary: discuss different types of accommodation and facilities
- Grammar: revise and extend comparisons
- Skills: work out and compare detail in information given

ESCUCHAR 1 🎧 **Escucha. Copia y completa la tabla.**
Listen to the five passages. Copy and complete the table.

lugar	alojamiento	opinión

Gramática → p.168

Comparatives – Comparing things
Can you remember how to say 'more than' / 'less than'? (See pages 91 and 98.)
Give two examples to show you know how to use these comparisons.

Another way to compare things is to use 'as ... as': *tan ... como*.
Una pensión es tan cómoda como un hotel.

Mejor que means 'better than': *El tren es mejor que el autobús.*
Peor que means 'worse than': *El autobús es peor que el coche.*

Good, better, best is *bueno, mejor, el / la / lo mejor*
Bad, worse, worst is *malo, peor, el / la / lo peor*

To say something is 'the best' or 'the worst':
Es una buena idea – en efecto es la mejor idea de todas.
No, no es una buena idea; es la peor idea de todas.
Es el mejor hotel del mundo.

Translate the examples into English.

? Think

What do you notice about the word *cómoda*? Which noun (*pensión* or *hotel*) does it agree with?

Now compare a campsite to a pension using the same adjective. What rule can you make about agreements when comparing things?

Compare the Spanish and English for the last example. Which key word is used differently?

VIDEO 2 🎥 **Mira el video y contesta a las preguntas.**
Watch the video and answer the questions.

1 What kind of accommodation is discussed?
2 What opinion does Khalid give?
3 Who else is going to come?

See Zoom OxBox

¿Tiene una piscina grande?

¿Hay canchas de tenis?

¿Hay ascensor?

¿Dónde están las duchas?

¿Me puede dar unas sábanas?

¿Tiene restaurante / cafetería?

¿Está cerca / lejos de la playa?

¿A qué hora podemos desayunar?

LEER 3

Empareja las preguntas con las respuestas.

Match the questions to the answers given below.

a Lo siento, no tenemos sábanas.
b Pues por supuesto hay ascensor.
c El comedor abre a las ocho en punto.
d Estamos a cien metros de la playa.
e Están al lado de la piscina a la izquierda.
f Hay tres detrás del hotel.
g Por supuesto hay una piscina grande.
h Tenemos un comedor en el interior y otro en la terraza.

una cancha
un ascensor
unas sábanas
una almohada

LEER 4

¿Verdad o mentira?

Is the receptionist in Activity 3 telling the truth?
Compare what is said with the information below.

HABLAR 5

Da tu opinión.

NC 3

Would you want to stay here? Give your opinion about the hotel and its facilities.

Ejemplo: (No) Me gusta el hotel porque…

? Think

Work out how best to sort out the detail of what is given in the hotel information, the questions customers ask and the answers the receptionist gives them.

Estimados clientes

Bienvenidos al hotel Miramar, el mejor hotel de la región.
Ofrecemos muchas facilidades para todos los gustos.

- El hotel está a varios kilómetros de la playa pero hay un autobús que sale cada quince minutos.
- Para los niños hay una piscina pequeña en el jardín. Hay una sola ducha detrás.
- Hay muchos restaurantes en la ciudad pero aquí les ofrecemos un bar con bebidas frías nada más.
- Los dormitorios están en el segundo piso. Pueden subir por las escaleras a la derecha de la recepción.
- Las sábanas están encima de las camas. Si necesitan más pueden pedirlas en recepción.
- Para los deportistas hay muchas facilidades en el polideportivo local.

Challenge

Write a brief paragraph about your ideal holiday accommodation – where it is, what it offers etc.

Swap papers with a partner who will then ask you questions based on the information written down. Use the questions from Activity 3 to help you. See how much you can remember about what you have written.

NC 4

 **See Zoom OxBox**

- Vocabulary: make a reservation
- Grammar: use formal and informal language correctly (*tú* and *usted*)
- Skills: create formal and informal dialogues of your own

Escucha y lee la conversación.

Listen and read the phone conversation.

- Oiga, ¿es el albergue juvenil Mundojoven?
- Sí, dígame.
- Quiero confirmar una reserva, por favor.
- El nombre, por favor.
- Rodríguez: R-O-D-R-I-G-U-E-Z.
- Vale. ¿Para cuántas personas?
- Para cinco: dos adultos y tres chicos.
- ¿Para cuándo?
- Desde el ocho hasta el veintiuno de julio.
- Gracias. Le confirmo: cinco personas del ocho al ...

Practica la conversación.

Practise the conversation with a partner.

Inventa otros diálogos.

Make up some more dialogues using the details on the right.

Lee y anota.

Your friend wants to know about the Mundojoven youth hostel.
Read the details and note down the answers to their questions.

1 How do I book?
2 What kind of rooms do they have?
3 What meals can I have there?
4 Are there any washing facilities?

5 Do I have to bring my own bed linen?
6 Is there internet access?
7 What time does it close?

Albergue juvenil Mundojoven

| FAQS | Fotos |

▶ ¿Reservaciones?	en línea, por email/teléfono o fax
▶ ¿Dormitorios?	de 4 a 12 camas sencillas; 4 habitaciones dobles
▶ ¿Comida?	desayuno gratis desde las 8:00 hasta las 10:00
▶ ¿Duchas?	gratis 24 horas al día
▶ ¿Ropa de cama?	no incluida; cada cama trae almohada y duvet
▶ ¿Internet?	WiFi gratis
▶ ¿Horario?	recepción 24 horas; entrada 12:00h; salida 11:00h

See Zoom OxBox

Escucha y pon la conversación en orden.

Listen to this dialogue on a campsite, and put speech bubbles a–h into the correct order.

a ¿Cuántas tiendas tenéis entre los cinco?

b Bueno, dime cuántas personas sois.

c Está bien; podéis acampar allá al lado de las duchas.

d Pues somos cinco personas.

e Sí, vamos a reservar una plaza.

f Tenemos tres: una para las dos chicas; otra para mis dos hermanos y una individual para mí.

g Vale. ¿Y cuántas noches vais a pasar en el camping?

h Vamos a pasar cuatro noches, del seis al nueve inclusive.

Oye, ¿vais a hacer camping aquí?

Escribe el diálogo y practícalo.

Write out the dialogue and practise it with a partner.

NC 2–3

Escucha la información y contesta a las preguntas.

Listen to the information and answer the questions.

1 What time is the café open?
2 Is it closed during winter?
3 What kind of food do they serve?
4 Where is it situated?
5 What else does it offer?

? Think

Una tienda has two different meanings; what are they?

? Think

Look back at pages 92 and 98. Compare the style and language of the two conversations.

Which one uses the more polite way of speaking?

What word do they both begin with?

Can you think of examples of similar language in English?

Write a letter, fax or email to book a holiday for your family in Sitges. State the number of people, dates of stay, rooms required and facilities. Add any further details you think important.

NC 3–4

See Zoom OxBox

3B.4 ¿Adónde vamos?

- Vocabulary: talk about what you are going to do on holiday
- Grammar: form and use adverbs correctly
- Skills: extend your writing by using a dictionary effectively

1 **Escucha y lee el diálogo.**
Listen and read the dialogue below.

> Vamos a dar una vuelta en autobús turístico. Pasan frecuentemente, cada media hora.
>
> No me gusta porque va muy lentamente – prefiero ir rápidamente.
>
> Así no aprecias nada. Podemos bajarnos en varias paradas y subir a otro autobús más tarde.
>
> Bueno, en autobús probablemente no nos perdemos.
>
> Normalmente comenzamos en la Plaza Catalunya.
>
> Vale, así nos encontramos fácilmente.

¡Esto es precioso!

Creo que es maravilloso.

2 **Mira el video-blog.**
Watch the video and note down the answers to the questions.

- ¿Qué te gusta hacer durante las vacaciones?
- ¿Adónde vas durante las vacaciones?
- ¿Cómo viajas?

3   **Escucha y contesta.**
Listen and answer the questions.
Who is going to ...

1 fly to America?
2 go camping?
3 stay at home?
4 stay in the mountains?
5 work in a shop over the holidays?

4 **Contesta a las preguntas sobre ti.**

NC 3

Answer the questions in Activity 2 for yourself.

5 **Escribe un párrafo.**

NC 3–4

Write a brief paragraph about what you are going to do during the holidays. Mention the following:

- el lugar y el alojamiento
- con quién vas a ir
- el transporte
- las actividades

Gramática → p.168

Adverbs
To form adverbs in Spanish, simply add the ending *-mente* onto the end of the adjective:
normal + *mente* = *normalmente* = normally
fácil + *mente* = *fácilmente* = easily
semanal + *mente* = *semanalmente* = weekly

How do you form adverbs in English?
What is the equivalent in English to the Spanish ending *-mente*?

If the adjective has a feminine form then you add the *-mente* ending to this.
rápido → *rápida* + *mente* = *rápidamente*
lento → *lenta* + *mente* = *lentamente*

- How many adverbs can you find in the dialogue above?

Some adverbs which do not follow this rule are:
siempre mucho poco bien mal bastante demasiado

See Zoom OxBox

VIDEO 6

 Mira el video.

Does Marisa like the idea of Eva joining them on their trip to Figueres? What do you think the two boys are scheming?

LEER 7

¿Qué tiene de especial Figueres?

Look at the information below and answer the questions.

1 Dalí was:
 a a teacher **b** a painter **c** a politician

2 Find the Spanish for:
 a children under nine
 b the rest of the year
 c the journey lasts one and a half hours
 d up to the present day

3 Complete the sentences.
 a Figueres está al ▨▨▨ de Barcelona y España.
 b El Museo Dalí abre ▨▨▨ los días en el verano.
 c Se puede coger un ▨▨▨ desde la estación de Sants.
 d Hay otros ▨▨▨ en Figueres.

? Think

Did you think this text was going to be difficult to understand at first? Did you need to translate every word to be able to get the gist of it?

Did the images help you? Are the headings helpful?

Try not to use a dictionary. Make connections to what you already know. For example, the word *juguetes* comes from the word *jugar* (to play) which you already know.

Now check how best to use a dictionary on page 115.

Challenge

Prepare a web page about a place of interest near your home or about what there is to do in your home area. If you need to, read page 115 to help you use your dictionary. **NC 4**

El Museo Dalí

Abierto cada día del uno de junio hasta el 30 de septiembre de 9h a 20h.

El resto del año abierto de 10:30h a 18h. Cerrado los lunes, el 25 de diciembre y el 1 de enero.

Niños menores de nueve años – gratis. Descuentos para estudiantes y jubilados.

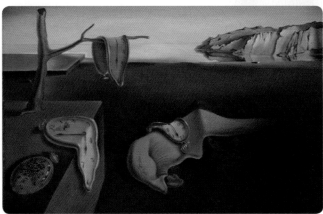

▌¿Dónde está? ¿Cómo llegar?

A aproximadamente 100 km al norte de Barcelona.
En tren, desde la estación de Sants o Gràcia, el viaje dura una hora y media.

FIGUERES
BARCELONA

▌Pintor y artista

Salvador Dalí nace en Figueres en 1904 y muere en 1989. Se casa con Gala – Elena Ivanova Diakanova.

▌Otros detalles de interés

El Museo del Joguet contiene más de cinco mil juguetes – algunos son del propio Dalí.
Museo Empordá explica la historia de la región desde los griegos hasta nuestros días.

▌Opiniones

❝ El surrealismo es algo fenomenal, me fascina la imaginación de Dalí. ❞

❝ Sus imágenes son inolvidables y geniales. Me encanta visitar el museo. ❞

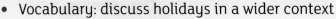

- Vocabulary: discuss holidays in a wider context
- Grammar: revise and extend language already covered
- Skills: be aware of cultural differences in the Spanish-speaking world

¿omóc?   ¿sotnáuc?   ¿éuq?   ¿néiuq?

¿láuc?

¿ednód?   ¿odnáuc?   ¿ednóda?   ¿rop éuq?

¿Cuántas preguntas puedes hacer?
How many question words do you know?
Who can make the longest list the fastest?

Copia y completa el diálogo.
Use the question words to complete
the dialogue.

? Think

Discuss why it is important to know these
question words.

Practica el diálogo.
Practise the dialogue with a partner.

NC 3

Lee la carta y busca las palabras.
Read Marisa's aunt's letter and find the
following words.

1 remember   4 in the countryside
2 for the rain   5 write soon
3 the twins

Analiza el texto.
Analyse the text of the letter in Activity 4 and
note down:

1 the verbs that are in the immediate future
2 the words for three family members
3 names for items of clothing
4 three adjectives

Escribe una carta de respuesta.
Write a letter of reply from Marisa to her aunt.

NC 4

Oye Marisa, ¿(1) ____ vas en Argentina?
Pues, voy a Buenos Aires y Bariloche.

¿(2) ____ vas a salir entonces?
Pronto, muy pronto.

¿(3) ____ tiempo vas a estar allí?
Creo que todo el mes de agosto.

¿(4) ____ vas a viajar?
Primero voy en tren hasta Madrid y luego salgo de
Barajas para Buenos Aires en avión.

¿(5) ____ tiempo hace en Buenos Aires en agosto?
Bueno, en Buenos Aires hace buen tiempo pero en
Bariloche hace un frío terrible en agosto; hay nieve –
pero mucha nieve.

¿(6) ____ vas a hacer en Bariloche?
Voy a esquiar y luego voy a ir en barco por los lagos y
voy a pasar la frontera hasta Chile.
¡Qué guay! ¡Qué aventura!

Querida Marisa

*Todos estamos super contentos porque vas a visitarnos
en agosto.*

*Acuérdate de que aquí en agosto es invierno y vas a
necesitar ropa adecuada: un impermeable para la lluvia y
un chandal o un jersey grueso para esquiar y para el frío.*

*Vamos a celebrar la primera comunión de tus primos,
los gemelos Oswaldo y Octavio, así que vas a comer tus
platos argentinos favoritos, bifechorizo con chimichurri.
Vamos a hacer un asado grande en el campo, en casa de
los abuelos.*

*Luego vas a ir con tu mamá a las montañas, a Bariloche.
¡Espero que te guste esquiar!*

*Escríbeme pronto con más preguntas sobre tus vacaciones
y dime lo que quieres hacer.*

Un abrazo fuerte

Tía Luchi

Lee y empareja.
Read Marisa's Facebook entry and match the photos and descriptions.

Escucha el guía. ¿Qué fotos describe?
Listen to the guide. Which three photos is he describing?

Argentina – agosto

Marisa

Queridos amigos, aquí os envío fotos de mis vacaciones en Argentina.

1 El Teatro Colón – restaurado y estupendo

2 Bailamos en la calle – empieza un festival de tango el 15 de agosto

3 El Puerto y el barrio de la Boca

4 La famosa Bombonera, el estadio de fútbol

5 En la Plaza de Mayo

6 Una clásica parrilla de carne asada

7 Las Estancias – el campo y los gauchos son parte de nuestra identidad.

8 Bariloche – ¡esquiando en agosto! ¿Qué tal?

? Think

Make a list of new words you have learnt on these pages and look them up in a dictionary. Check out the advice on page 115 before you do so.

Study the words for a few minutes then test yourself with a partner. Who can remember the most?

Challenge
Write some real or imaginary details about a trip you are going to make.

NC 4–5

Comprender – Verb tenses and adverbs

A Tenses

The word 'tense' means time. The tense tells you when in a time sequence the action of the verb used takes place: is it **past**, **present** or **future**?

So far you have used verbs in the present tense only. In this unit you have learnt to form the **immediate future**, which tells you what is **going** to happen or what you are **going** to do.

Take the verb *ir + a* + the **infinitive** of the verb of action.

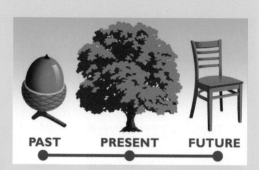

PAST   PRESENT   FUTURE

Voy a comer a la una	Vamos a ir de vacaciones
Vas a nadar en la piscina	Vais a viajar a Colombia
Va a salir con sus amigos	Van a jugar al baloncesto

1 Translate the sentences above into English.

Remind yourself about **reflexive** verbs (see pages 60 and 66). When you use a reflexive verb like *levantarse* (to get up) remember to keep the reflexive pronoun attached to the end of the infinitive. You also have to remember to change the reflexive pronoun so it agrees with the person doing the verb.

Voy a levantar**me**	= yo
Vas a levantar**te**	= tú
Va a levantar**se**	= él / ella / usted
Vamos a levantar**nos**	= nosotros
Vais a levantar**os**	= vosotros
Van a levantar**se**	= ellos / ellas / ustedes

B Adverbs

Adverbs are used to describe the action of a verb. They **do not** agree with the verb, so unlike adjectives they **do not change**.

Examples:

normal + mente = normalmente
rápido – rápida + mente = rápidamente

2 **Write out these sentences correctly.**

Example: Voy a (levantarse) temprano. = Voy a levantarme temprano.

1 Vamos a (despertarse) tarde mañana.
2 Voy a (acostarse) a las diez esta noche.
3 ¿Vas a (ponerse) los vaqueros y una camiseta?
4 ¿Vosotros vais a (bañarse) en la piscina?
5 Amalia y Rosita van a (lavarse) el pelo.

3 There are some useful adverbs which do not end like this. Unscramble these other adverbs.

> prisme   humco   coop   ineb   lam   tasbetan   masidamdo

Make up a sentence for each to show you know what they mean.

See Zoom OxBox

Aprender – Extending sentences

C Connectives, reasons, and using your dictionary

Remember that to reach a higher level in your work you need to get into the habit of speaking or writing longer sentences.

So far you have learnt how to extend sentences using **connectives** such as *pero, sin embargo, en cambio* and *también*.

Also you can give **opinions** or **reasons** such as ... *porque me gusta / me encanta / me fastidia / me aburre* etc.

In Unit 2B you used a lot more **adjectives** to help make your work more interesting.

In this unit you have learnt how to form and use **adverbs** to help you make the verbs used more interesting.

In order to become a more independent and reflective learner you need to be sure about how to use a dictionary.

4 **How well do you know your way around your dictionary?**
What do these letters mean? n m f adj vb
Find five more sets of letters in your dictionary and learn what they mean.

5 **Don't forget that words often have more than one meaning!**
How many meanings does the word 'pool' have in English?

Can you think of two meanings for the word *café* in Spanish?

Remember to check (by comparing Spanish/English with English/ Spanish) that words you choose from your dictionary are really the ones you want!

6 **Now look up the verb *hacer* and find out all the meanings and examples of the way this verb can be used.**

Hablar – Pronunciation

D Speaking fluently and sounding really Spanish

When a word ends with a vowel and the next word also begins with a vowel Spanish people tend to slide the two words together.

7 🎧 **Listen and practise saying:**

Anita y Amalia‿aprenden a‿hablar italiano.
José‿e‿Inés van a‿escribir una carta‿a‿Alberto.
This is called *sinalefa*.

8 🎧 **Listen and work out which words slide into each other.**

Los otros amigos van a alojarse en los hoteles más baratos.
Vamos a Buenos Aires en un avión de Iberia.

When consonants also slide into the next word, it is called *entrelazamiento*.

▶ *See Zoom OxBox*

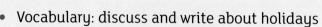

- Vocabulary: discuss and write about holidays
- Grammar: use the immediate future and adverbs correctly
- Skills: write longer sentences

ESCUCHAR 1

NC 3–4

Escucha. Copia y completa la tabla.
Listen to the people describing their holiday plans.
Copy and complete the table.

	¿Adónde va?	¿Cómo va?	¿Alojamiento?	¿Opinión?
José				
María				
Roberto				
Raquel				

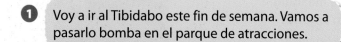

divertido/a   aburrido/a   genial   fatal   sensacional
guay   bomba

LEER 2

NC 2–3

Lee y empareja.
Read the texts and match them with the photos.
There is one extra photo.

1 Voy a ir al Tibidabo este fin de semana. Vamos a pasarlo bomba en el parque de atracciones.

2 Voy al Mercado de la Boquería porque quiero comprar comida típica.

3 Vamos al Parque Güell y a la Sagrada Familia porque quiero ver lo extraordinario que es Gaudí.

4 Quiero visitar el Barrio Gótico y ver la parte antigua de la ciudad.

HABLAR 3

NC 3

Prepara una presentación oral sobre un viaje.
Prepare an oral presentation about a journey you are going to make. Choose three of the following questions to answer.

- ¿Adónde vas a ir?
- ¿Con quién vas a ir?
- ¿Cómo vas a viajar?
- ¿A qué hora vas a salir?
- ¿Dónde vas a alojarte?

- ¿Qué ropa vas a ponerte?
- ¿Qué quieres comer y beber?
- ¿Qué vas a hacer?
- ¿Qué vas a visitar?

See Zoom OxBox

- Vocabulary: read and understand tourist information
- Grammar: convert commands to infinitives
- Skills: listen for detailed information

 ESCUCHAR 1

 Escucha y anota. Copia y completa la tabla.

NC 4

	¿Dónde?	¿Cuánto tiempo?	¿Transporte?	¿Alojamiento?	¿Actividades?
Sebas					
Anita		—			
Maripacha					
Julián					

 ESCUCHAR 2

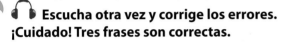 **Escucha otra vez y corrige los errores.**
¡Cuidado! Tres frases son correctas.

NC 4

1 Sebas va a ir a Sevilla.
2 Va a quedarse en casa de su tío.
3 Anita quiere ir a la playa.
4 Quiere hacer surf y nadar.

5 Maripacha va con su familia a Méjico.
6 Van a pasar un mes allí.
7 Julián va a ir a pie a Santiago de Compostela.
8 Va a quedarse en albergues juveniles.

 HABLAR 3

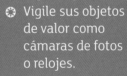 **Lee el informe turístico.**
Explica lo que tienes que hacer.

NC 3–4

*Ejemplo: Tienes que ... **seguir** las recomendaciones.*

 ESCRIBIR 4

Planea una visita a Isla Mágica. Escribe un texto sobre lo que vas a hacer. Usa las preguntas de la Actividad 3 (página 116) para ayudarte.

NC 4–5

Isla Mágica, Sevilla

Gracias por su visita.

¡Bienvenidos a la Sagrada Familia!

Para disfrutar de su visita siga las recomendaciones de abajo:

- Reserve su entrada.
- Compre una guía para orientarse mejor.
- Guarde su pasaporte y su dinero en un lugar seguro.
- Vigile sus objetos de valor como cámaras de fotos o relojes.
- Suba a la torre con mucho cuidado.
- Visite la tumba de Gaudí en la cripta.
- Siga la ruta indicada.
- Observe las normas, por favor.

Escuchar

NC 3

Listen and write down the most appropriate answer.

1 Tomás va a visitar Sevilla / Bilbao / Madrid.
2 Va a viajar en avión / tren / coche.
3 Va a alojarse en un hotel / un albergue juvenil / un camping.
4 Va a quedarse cerca del puerto / del estadio / de la catedral.
5 Quiere comprar regalos / comida típica / una guitarra.
6 Va a comer tapas / pescado / helados.
7 Va a esquiar / montar a caballo / hacer surf.
8 Las vacaciones van a ser aburridas / bastante buenas / las mejores.

Hablar

NC 3–4

Describe an imaginary trip to Figueres or Barcelona. Give the following information:

- when you are going to go
- who you are going with
- how you are going to travel
- what you want to do there
- what you want to eat and drink there
- what you are going to wear

Leer

NC 3–4

Read the information and answer these questions in English.

1 Where is this landmark centre?
2 How many different buildings does it consist of?
3 What is different about the science exhibition?
4 What can you do in the Oceanografic centre?
5 What kind of services are available?
6 What do they recommend you buy?
7 Who can get a reduced entry ticket?

Escribir

NC 4–5

Write an account of an imaginary day trip to the Ciudad de las Artes y las Ciencias in Valencia. Think about what you are going to do there, how you are going to get there, etc.

 **La Ciudad de las Artes y las Ciencias – Valencia**

Museo de Ciencias Príncipe Felipe – Prohibido *no* tocar: un nuevo concepto de museo donde participar y experimentar con la ciencia y la tecnología actual y del futuro.

L'Oceanografic – El mayor centro marino de Europa; un viaje submarino para descubrir los encantos y secretos de los mares y océanos.

L'Hemisferic – Original edificio con forma de ojo humano. Tres espectáculos audiovisuales diferentes en una pantalla de gran formato: Planetario, IMAX y Laserium.

El Palacio de las Artes – Emblema de las artes escénicas. Un centro pionero donde se programan los mejores espectáculos de danza, ópera y teatro.

Servicios
Todos los servicios necesarios para que todo el mundo se lo pase bien.

Tiendas, aparcamientos, áreas de descanso, espacios para niños, cafeterías y restaurantes.

Compra tu entrada "La Ciutat" y disfruta de todo el complejo al mejor precio.

Tarifa reducida para niños menores de 12 años. Pensionistas, jubilados y personas discapacitadas.

15% descuento para estudiantes. Entrada gratuita para niños de 0–4 años.

 **See Zoom OxBox**

El transporte	Transport
en autobús (el)	by bus
en metro (el)	by underground
en barco (el)	by boat
en bicicleta (la)	by bike
en tren (el)	by train
en avión (el)	by plane
en coche (el)	by car
en autocar (el)	by coach
un viaje	a journey
viajar	to travel
cómodo/a	comfortable
barato/a	cheap
corto/a	short
divertido/a	amusing
un billete	a ticket
ida y vuelta	return
cada veinte minutos	every 20 minutes
tardar	to take time

Alojamiento	Accommodation
alojarse	to board/to stay
un albergue juvenil	youth hostel
una pensión	bed and breakfast
un camping	campsite
quedarse	to stay
vale la pena	it's worth it
antiguo/a	ancient/old
tan ... como	as ... as
mejor	better
el / la mejor	the best
peor	worse
el / la peor	the worst
la sábana	sheet
la habitación	bedroom
el ascensor	lift

Quiero reservar ...	I want to reserve ...
reservar	to reserve/to book
una reserva	a booking
confirmar	to confirm
incluido/a	included
el precio	the price
cerrar	to close
cerrado/a	closed
abrir	to open
abierto/a	open
una plaza	a camping plot
una tienda	a tent
inclusive	inclusive
acampar	to pitch a tent

¿Adónde vamos?	Where shall we go?
precioso/a	pretty
maravilloso/a	marvellous
cada	each/every
media hora	half hour
apreciar	to appreciate
una parada	stop (bus)
perderse	to get lost
encontrarse	to meet/find each other
el dinero	money
tener suerte	to be lucky
menores de	under the age of
la estación	station
nace	is born
se casa con	marries
un juguete	toy
inolvidable	unforgettable
divertido/a	amusing
genial	great
fatal	awful
sensacional	amazing
guay	great
pasarlo bomba	to have a great time
un parque de atracciones	fun fair/theme park
el mercado	market
antiguo/a	ancient
un guía	a guide (person)
una guía	a guide book
orientarse	to find your way
guardar	to keep (safe)
vigilar	to look after
una torre	tower
una tumba	tomb
las normas	rules and regulations

◉ I can ...

- ◉ use comparisons correctly
- ◉ use the immediate future
- ◉ talk about means of transport
- ◉ book a holiday in a hotel or campsite
- ◉ talk about different holiday activities and places

- Vocabulary: say what can/can't be done in your region and why
- Grammar: use *(no) se puede* correctly
- Skills: avoid repetition of common vocabulary

Se puede jugar al fútbol

No se puede jugar al fútbol

 ESCUCHAR 1

🎧 **Escucha. ¿Qué se puede hacer en Zaragoza?**
Listen. Match the photos to the places, then listen again and list the photos in the order they are mentioned.

Ejemplo: 1 b La Seo

La Misericordia   El Río Ebro   La Romareda   La Seo
El Parque Metropolitano del Agua   El Parque Grande
La Aljafería   El Mercado Central

? **Think**

Listen again, focusing on the verbs that follow the expression *se puede*. What do they have in common?

a

b

c

d

e

f

g

h

See Zoom OxBox

2 Une las dos partes de las frases. En Zaragoza ...

Match the two parts of the sentences so that they make sense.

Ejemplo: 1 c

1 Se puede comer bien ...
2 No se puede ir a la playa ...
3 Se puede continuar estudiando ...
4 Se puede ir de compras ...
5 Se puede visitar la ciudad sin necesidad de un coche ...
6 Se puede hacer deporte al aire libre ...

a ... pues hay una universidad muy buena.
b ... porque hay parques y polideportivos con espacio exterior.
c ... porque hay una gran variedad de restaurantes.
d ... ya que lamentablemente no hay mar.
e ... porque hay muchas tiendas y centros comerciales.
f ... puesto que el transporte público es muy bueno.

3 Escribe las frases de la Actividad 2 en su sentido contrario.

Rewrite the sentences in Activity 2 so they have the opposite meaning. Remember! To make the negative in Spanish you need to put the word *no* immediately in front of the verb.

*Ejemplo: **No** se puede comer bien porque no hay mucha variedad de restaurantes.*

4 Hablar. En dos equipos debéis llegar a la meta.

NC 3

Speaking. In two teams you must go from left to right or from top to bottom, taking turns to say grammatically correct sentences that make sense. You can choose your starting hexagon but after that you can only choose a hexagon that touches the previous one.

Se puede ...
porque hay ...

No se puede ...
porque no hay ...

? Think

To improve the quality of your speaking and writing avoid repetition. How many different ways of saying 'because' can you find in Activity 2?

Gramática → p.164

Se puede

Se puede is an impersonal expression that means 'one can'/'one is allowed'. However, we often translate it as 'you can'/'you are allowed'.

It **must** be followed by an infinitive:

jugar

Se puede + *comer*

beber

Challenge

Write a paragraph about what you can/can't do in your city and why.

NC 3–4

4A.2 ¿Adónde fuiste?

- Vocabulary: talk about the weather in the past tense
- Grammar: use the verb *ir* correctly in the preterite
- Skills: link sentences to avoid repetition

 **Think**

How would you say ...
five years ago? last week?
last January?

 Mira el video. ¿Adónde fueron Eva y Marisa de vacaciones? ¿Con quién fueron?
Watch the video. Where did Eva and Marisa go on holiday? Who did they go with?

 ¿Cuándo? Empareja estas expresiones con su significado.
When? Match these phrases with the correct meaning.

Ejemplo: 1 b

1	el verano pasado	a	two years ago
2	el invierno pasado	b	last summer
3	el año pasado	c	last Christmas
4	hace dos años	d	last winter
5	el pasado junio	e	last June
6	las Navidades pasadas	f	last year

 Lee. ¿Verdadero o falso? Corrige las frases falsas.
Read. True or false? Correct the incorrect sentences.

1 Generalmente Eva y su familia van a Méjico.
2 El año pasado Eva fue a Méjico con sus tíos.
3 Viajaron a Méjico en barco.
4 En Méjico generalmente hace buen tiempo.
5 Durante sus vacaciones hizo frío.
6 Un día estuvo nublado y nevó.

¡Hola! Soy Eva. Normalmente voy de vacaciones a Italia con mis padres porque nos gusta mucho la cultura, visitar museos etc. Pero el año pasado, como sabéis, fuimos a Méjico porque mis padres vivieron allí cuando eran estudiantes y querían volver. Claro, fuimos en avión porque está demasiado lejos para ir en barco. Afortunadamente en Méjico casi siempre hace bueno así que durante las vacaciones hizo sol y mucho calor.
Un día estuvo nublado, llovió y por la noche hubo tormenta.

 **Gramática** → p.166

Past and present of the verb *ir*

Present:	Past:
voy *(I go)*	fui *(I went)*
vas *(you go)*	fuiste *(you went)*
va *(he/she/it goes)*	fue *(he/she/it went)*
vamos *(we go)*	fuimos *(we went)*
vais *(you pl. go)*	fuisteis *(you pl. went)*
van *(they go)*	fueron *(they went)*

Normalmente **voy** de vacaciones a Málaga.
*Normally **I go** on holiday to Malaga.*

El año pasado **fui** a Barcelona. *Last year **I went** to Barcelona.*

See Zoom OxBox

LEER 4

Copia y completa la tabla.
Use the text in Activity 3 to work out the past tenses.

		present	past
		Hace calor	
		Hace viento	
	☺	Hace buen tiempo	
		Está nublado	
		Hay tormenta	
		Hay niebla	
		Llueve	

🎧 **Escucha y decide si es en pasado o en presente.**
Listen and decide if it's in the past or present.

Challenge

👥 Throw a dice six times and note the sequence (e.g. 322464). Don't let your partner see! Write the sentence in Spanish: work your way from A to F using the number sequence to choose from 1 to 6 in each line. Then read the complete sentence to your partner who must work out your sequence.

Ejemplo: =

El año pasado fuiste a los Estados Unidos en barco con tus padres. Hizo viento.

	1	2	3	4	5	6
A ¿Cuándo?			Last year	2 years ago	August	🎄
B ¿Quién?	yo	tú	él	nosotros	vosotros	ellos
C ¿Adónde?						
D ¿Cómo?						
E ¿Con quién?				OR		
F ¿Qué tiempo hizo?	☀		☁		☂	

NC 5

? Think

Avoid repetition and extend your sentences to achieve a higher level.

For example:
El año pasado <u>fuiste</u> a los Estados Unidos. <u>Fuiste</u> en barco. <u>Fuiste</u> con tus padres. Hizo viento. → *El año pasado **fuiste** a los Estados Unidos en barco con tus padres. Hizo viento.*

⚙ *Gramática* → p.163

Remember!

Personal pronouns	Possessive adjectives
yo	mi/mis
yú	tu/tus
él/ella	su/sus
nosotros(as)	nuestro(a)/nuestros(as)
vosotros(as)	vuestro(a)/vuestros(as)
ellos(as)	su/sus

- Vocabulary: talk about free time activities in the past tense
- Grammar: use the preterite of regular verbs correctly
- Skills: write about someone else

El invierno pasado fui de vacaciones a Chile con mis tíos. Fuimos en avión y nos alojamos en un camping porque es más barato. En Chile era verano así que la mayoría de las tardes tomé el sol y me bañé en la playa con mi primo. Después, por la noche, comimos comidas típicas en restaurantes de la zona. El lunes hice vela con el club náutico y el miércoles hice surf. ¡Uff!
¡Es muy difícil!

Ana María

El año pasado fui con mi familia a Dublín donde hizo frío todos los días menos el jueves que hizo sol, así que nos relajamos al lado de la piscina.
El lunes visitamos los museos y paseamos por las calles. Saqué muchas fotos. El martes me quedé en el hotel y leí una revista porque llovía y el miércoles salí de compras y compré unos recuerdos.
El viernes, antes de volver a casa, escribí unas postales a mis amigos.

Charo

LEER 1

Lee lo que dicen Ana María y Charo. Escribe las letras.
Read what Ana María and Charo say.
Write the letters of the activities each mentions.

a   b   c   d   e   f
g   h   i   j   k   l

LEER 2

Pon las palabras en la sección correspondiente del diagrama.
Copy the spider diagram and place the words in the box in the appropriate section.

surf   un hotel   fruta   comida típica   calor   los deberes
un museo   unas postales   avión   Dinamarca   paella
un albergue juvenil   recuerdos   barco   la piscina   vela
un camping   Canadá   buen tiempo   castillo   unos CDs
muchas ensaladas   casa de mis abuelos   moto   ciclismo
una exposición de arte   un centro comercial   una revista
las ruinas romanas   bicicleta   viento   sol

me alojé en
hizo
fui a
fui en
PRETÉRITO
hice
surf
comí
visité
compré

See Zoom OxBox

Gramática → p.165

The preterite tense

For regular verbs, take the infinitive ending off and replace it with the correct ending. But beware! Make sure you are looking at a preterite table as this will look similar to the present tense table.

Irregular verbs have their own particular conjugation.

Pronombres personales (Who?)		Irregular	Regular		
		to do/ to make **HACER**	*Ejemplo:* **VISITAR** –AR	*Ejemplo:* **COMER** –ER	*Ejemplo:* **ESCRIBIR** –IR
Singular	yo *(I)*	hice	visité	comí	escribí
	tú *(you)*	hiciste	visitaste	comiste	escribiste
	él/ella *(he/she)*	hizo	visitó	comió	escribió
Plural	nosotros/as *(we)*	hicimos	visitamos	comimos	escribimos
	vosotros/as *(you)*	hicisteis	visitasteis	comisteis	escribisteis
	ellos/as *(they)*	hicieron	visitaron	comieron	escribieron

3 **Identifica los verbos en pretérito. ¿Qué significan?**

Identify the verbs in the preterite in what Ana María and Charo say on page 124. What do they mean?

Ejemplo: Ana María: fui – I went, fuimos – we went, nos alojamos – we stayed ...

4 **Escucha. ¿Qué contestaron los chicos?**

Listen. What were these young people's replies to the reporter's questions?

- ¿Adónde fuiste?
- ¿Con quién fuiste?
- ¿Cómo viajaste?
- ¿Dónde te alojaste?
- ¿Qué tiempo hizo?
- ¿Qué hiciste allí?

5  **Hablar. Utiliza las preguntas del reportero para hacer un sondeo en la clase.**

NC 4–5

Use the reporter's questions in Activity 4 to interview your classmates about their last holiday.

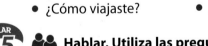

Think

Remember that when you are talking about someone else, it is not only the verbs you need to change but also possessive adjectives such as 'my' or 'our' for 'his/her' or 'their'.

Think

The main use of Spanish accents is to help with pronunciation as they tell the speaker which syllable of a word should be stressed. However, sometimes they may change the meaning of a word altogether and so it is imperative that you include them and pronounce them correctly.

visito – I visit   *visitó* – he visited

Challenge

Choose either Ana María's or Charo's paragraph and rewrite it in the third person.

*Example: (Ana María) El invierno pasado **fue** de vacaciones a Chile con **sus** hermanos. **Fueron** en avión y **se alojaron** ...*

NC 5

See Zoom OxBox

- Vocabulary: give your views on a past holiday
- Grammar: use opinions in the preterite tense
- Skills: turn Level 4 spoken or written work into Level 5

Hace dos años fui de vacaciones a Cuba y **lo pasé fenomenal**. Cuba es la isla más grande del Caribe y en mi opinión es la más bonita. Fui en avión y el viaje duró diez horas. **¡Qué aburrido!** Pasé unos días en La Habana, la capital, donde me alojé en un hotel en el Malecón, el largo paseo que bordea el mar. En mi opinión el hotel **fue regular** pero el Malecón es muy bonito.

En Cuba hay música en todas partes: tocan salsa en todos los bares y restaurantes y bailé en la discoteca casi todas las noches. **¡Lo pasé bomba!**

Durante las vacaciones hizo calor así que tomé el sol, descansé y practiqué deportes acuáticos como el esquí acuático y el buceo. ¡El esquí acuático **me encantó**!

También pasé unos días en el campo del Pinar del Río donde monté a caballo y visité una plantación de tabaco. Mi estancia en el campo **no estuvo mal** y **me gustó** montar a caballo.

Antes de volver a casa volví a La Habana y el último día fui de compras. Compré una camiseta de Che Guevara para mi hermano, una caja de cigarros habanos para mi padre y ron para mi abuelo aunque me olvidé la botella en el autobús. **¡Qué desastre!** La última noche vi un partido de béisbol que **fue muy emocionante**.

¡La verdad es que mis vacaciones **fueron increíbles**!

Alicia

Lee y empareja.
Read the text and match the expressions **in bold** with these English ones.

Ejemplo: 1 me gustó

1 I liked
2 They were unbelievable.
3 I had a blast!
4 It wasn't bad.
5 I had a great time.

6 It was very exciting.
7 It was average.
8 What a disaster!
9 I loved it!
10 How boring!

? Think

This passage would clearly be a comfortable Level 5. Can you explain why? How could it be turned into a Level 6?

See Zoom OxBox

LEER 2 Lee de nuevo. Contesta a las preguntas en inglés.

Read the text again and answer the questions in English.

1 When did Alicia go to Cuba?
2 Why was the journey boring?
3 What is *El Malecón*?
4 Why does she say she had a blast?
5 What did she do during her holiday?

6 What did she do in the countryside?
7 What gifts did she buy?
8 What was a disaster?
9 What did she do on her last night?
10 What's her opinion of her holiday?

VIDEO 3 Mira el video-blog. ¿Qué contestan los chicos a estas preguntas?

Watch the video blog. How do these young people answer the questions? Listen and make notes.

- ¿Adónde fuiste durante las vacaciones pasadas?
- ¿Qué hiciste?
- ¿Cómo viajaste?
- ¿Lo pasaste bien?

ESCUCHAR 4 Escucha y decide qué dibujo se describe: a, b o c.

Listen and decide which of the pictures is being described.

HABLAR 5 Elabora frases sobre las vacaciones. Utiliza los otros dibujos.

NC 4–5

Make up sentences about the other pictures.

 **Gramática →** p.166

Fue *regular* and **fueron** *increíbles* both come from the verb *ser.*

No **estuvo** *mal* comes from the verb *estar.*

Both *ser* and *estar* are irregular verbs; this means that they do not follow the pattern regular verbs do. Check page 130 to find out more.

? Think

Enhancing your speaking and writing with descriptions, quantifiers, connectives and lots of opinions gets you a higher level.

Ensure there is more than one time frame for a Level 5. For example, say where you normally go before saying where you went last year.

You could even get a Level 6 if the quality of your speaking or writing is good and you have used three time frames. You could for example say where you are going to go next year and why.

Challenge

Write a detailed description of a past holiday.

NC 5–6

- Vocabulary: practise language for buying souvenirs in a Spanish-speaking country

un abanico   un sombrero   unas gafas de sol

una camiseta

un vestido de flamenco

un llavero

un imán

una guitarra española

unas castañuelas   una muñeca

Escucha. ¿Qué compraron? ¿Para quién?
Listen. What did they buy? Who for?

Ejemplo: 1 e, hermana

¿Recuerdas los números? Empareja estos precios con su etiqueta.
Do you remember the Spanish numbers? Match these prices with their price tag.

Ejemplo: 1 c

1 Ocho euros cincuenta
2 Tres euros veinte
3 Diez euros noventa y nueve
4 Cinco euros cuarenta

5 Treinta y dos euros cincuenta
6 Doce euros veinticinco
7 Un euro noventa y nueve
8 Veintiocho euros sesenta

a 28,60€
b 1,99€
c 8,50€
d 32,50€
e 5,40€
f 12,25€
g 3,20€
h 10,99€

? Think

Remember that even words that look English need to be pronounced as Spanish words!
euros: [yuros] ✗   [eh-oo-ros] ✓

See Zoom OxBox

LEER 3

NC 3–4

Completa la conversación.
Re-write this conversation by putting the customer's part in the correct order.

Buenos días. ¿Qué deseas?

....

Hay este abanico rojo. Es muy bonito. ¿Te gusta?

....

Cuesta 25,99€.

....

Hmmm ... Tenemos imanes y llaveros.

....

3,50€. ¡Mira! ¿Te gusta?

....

¿Algo más?

....

Gracias, adiós.

....

- Quiero un regalo para mi abuela.
- Sí, me gusta. Me lo quedo.
- ¡Uy! ¡Es muy caro! No tengo suficiente dinero. ¿Tiene algo más barato?
- Sí, es bonito. ¿Cuánto cuesta?
- Adiós.
- No, nada más, gracias. 3,50€ ... aquí tiene.
- Un llavero, por favor. ¿Cuánto cuesta?

LEER 4

Busca el español.
Find the Spanish in the conversation.

1 What would you like?
2 I want
3 for my grandmother
4 How much is it?
5 It is very expensive.
6 Do you have anything cheaper?
7 Look! Do you like it?
8 I'll take it.
9 Anything else?
10 No, nothing else.

Challenge

Practise the conversation with a partner.

- Dependiente: Buenos días. ¿Qué deseas?
  Greet the shopkeeper and say you would like a souvenir for your mum/brother/friend.
- Dependiente: Hay estos imanes. Son muy bonitos y baratos. ¿Te gustan?
  Say you don't like them. You want castanets/a t-shirt/a key ring.
- Dependiente: ¡Mira! Las castañuelas/la camiseta/el llavero cuesta(n) 12,99€.
  Say it is/they are very expensive and ask if he/she has something cheaper.
- Dependiente: Sí, éstos/as son más baratos/as.
  Ask the price.
- Dependiente: Cuesta(n) 5,99€.
  Say you'll take it/them.
- Dependiente: ¿Algo más?
  Say you don't want anything else and thank the shopkeeper.
- Dependiente: Gracias, adiós.
  Say goodbye.

NC 4

Comprender – The multiple kingdoms of verbs (preterite)

A Regular verbs

To form the preterite of regular verbs follow the same rules as for the present tense, making sure you are looking at a preterite table.

If a verb is reflexive, e.g. *alojarse*, keep the *me, te, se, nos, os* or *se* pronoun and work out the rest as if it were a normal regular verb:

alojarse to stay   *me alojo* I stay   *me alojé* I stayed

Pronombres personales (Who?)		Regular		
		−AR Ejemplo: **hablar** (to speak)	−ER Ejemplo: **aprender** (to learn)	−IR Ejemplo: **vivir** (to live)
Singular	yo	hablé	aprendí	vivo
	tú	hablaste	aprendiste	viviste
	él/ella	habló	aprendió	vivió
Plural	nosotros/as	hablamos	aprendimos	vivimos
	vosotros/as	hablasteis	aprendisteis	vivisteis
	ellos/as	hablaron	aprendieron	vivieron

B Irregular verbs

Remember: irregular verbs don't follow the same rules.

ser SER	estar ESTAR	ir −IR	hacer HACER
fui	estuve	fui	hice
fuiste	estuviste	fuiste	hiciste
fue	estuvo	fue	hizo
fuimos	estuvimos	fuimos	hicimos
fuisteis	estuvisteis	fuisteis	hicisteis
fueron	estuvieron	fueron	hicieron

Look at the table. Do you notice anything unusual?

3 Complete the sentences with the preterite of the verb in brackets.

1 El año pasado mi madre y yo _____ a Buenos Aires. (ir)
2 Mi padre no _____ con nosotros porque trabajó todo el verano. (ir)
3 En Argentina _____ buen tiempo. (hacer)
4 La comida no _____ mal. (estar)

1 How do you say the following in Spanish?

1 to visit
2 to cook
3 to eat
4 to drink
5 to see
6 to go for a walk
7 to sunbathe
8 to take photos
9 to buy
10 to stay

2 Translate:

1 I visited
2 we cooked
3 you ate
4 she drank
5 we saw
6 they went for a walk
7 I sunbathed
8 you (plural) took pictures
9 you (formal) bought
10 we stayed

4 Rewrite this paragraph in the preterite. Remember to change the time markers where necessary.

Todos los años voy de vacaciones a Mijas, cerca de Málaga. Voy con mis abuelos en avión y nos alojamos en un apartamento de alquiler. En Mijas hace buen tiempo y hace mucho calor. Durante las vacaciones vamos a la playa, nos bañamos en el mar y nos relajamos al lado de la piscina. También comemos comida típica en restaurantes del pueblo. ¡Siempre lo paso fenomenal!

Aprender – Writing or talking about past events

C Time markers

Whether you are speaking or writing it is important that you make it clear whether something has already happened, is happening at the moment or is going to happen in the future. After all, you don't want your potential date to think that you still watch the Teletubbies when what you wanted to say was that you liked them when you were three!

There are two ways of making this clear:

- By using time words or phrases that situate the action in time: *ayer* (yesterday), *hoy* (today), *mañana* (tomorrow).
- By the use of tenses: *tomo el sol* (present), *tomé el sol* (past), *voy a tomar el sol* (future).

5 Place these time phrases in three categories depending on whether they refer to past, present or future. Be careful: some may apply to more than one time frame.

ahora	el viernes pasado	en estos momentos
hoy	ayer	el martes
el verano pasado	la semana pasada	mañana por la mañana
los sábados	anteayer	el próximo año

6 Complete these sentences with the first person present, past or future of the verb *ir* accordingly.

1 Normalmente _____ de vacaciones a Dinamarca pero el año pasado _____ a Inglaterra.

2 Anteayer _____ al cine con mi primo, pero el próximo sábado no _____ al cine; _____ a ver un partido de fútbol.

3 _____ al gimnasio esta tarde porque ayer no _____ .

4 Anteayer _____ a la playa con mi hermana aunque generalmente sólo _____ a la playa en verano.

5 Ahora _____ al polideportivo dos veces a la semana, pero el próximo año _____ todos los días.

Hablar – Pronunciation

D Accents

For non-native speakers, it can be difficult to grasp just how important accents on Spanish letters are. They don't only change the pronunciation of a word, but can actually change the entire meaning.

compro – *I buy*	compró – *he bought*
si – *if*	sí – *yes*
bebe – *he drinks*	bebé – *baby*

7 🎧 Say the words on the left out loud. Check the recording.

8 Read these sentences out loud:

1 El lunes mi amiga compró un libro, pero yo nunca compro libros.

2 Ayer mi hermano no visitó a mis abuelos, pero yo les visito todos los días.

- Skills: find out about Spanish festivals

ESCRIBIR 1
NC 3

¿Qué se puede y no se puede hacer?
What can you and can you not do?

Ejemplo: 1 Se puede jugar al fútbol.

El encierro

La corrida

Los cabezudos

Los Sanfermines

Hola, soy Kieran. Normalmente voy de vacaciones a Tenerife con mi familia, pero el verano pasado fui a la fiesta de los Sanfermines.

Fui con mis amigos. Fuimos en avión desde Gatwick. Me alojé en un hotel en el centro de Pamplona. Durante la fiesta de los Sanfermines vi un encierro, una corrida, los cabezudos, el chupinazo y fui a una verbena.

Me gustaron mucho el encierro y el chupinazo pero no me gustó la corrida porque en mi opinión es cruel.

El año próximo no voy a volver a los Sanfermines porque voy a visitar a mi familia en Escocia.

LEER 2
NC 3–4

Lee y busca el español.
Read and find the Spanish.

1 I go on holiday to …
2 I went to the festival of San Fermín
3 with my friends
4 During the festival
5 I saw the bullrun
6 a bullfight
7 I liked … a lot
8 but I did not like …
9 in my opinion
10 Next year I am not going to return to …
11 because I am going to visit …

los cabezudos: *carnival figures with a very large head that are generally taken out to dance around in Spanish festivals. Each town and city has its own.*

el chupinazo: *a loud rocket shot to denote the start of the festival*

la verbena: *an evening street party very common in Spanish festivals*

ESCRIBIR 3
NC 3–4

Investigación cultural. Busca información sobre los Sanfermines.
Cultural research. Use the internet to find out about the San Fermín festival. Make a display poster with the key information.

See Zoom OxBox

- Skills: find out about Spanish festivals

La Tomatina

Cada año, **a finales de agosto**, turistas de todo el mundo van de vacaciones a Buñol, un pueblo mediterráneo al oeste de Valencia. **El verano pasado** yo también fui con mis amigos. Fuimos desde Barcelona en coche y tardamos unas tres horas y media. Allí nos alojamos en un hotel cerca del centro del pueblo. **Durante la semana** visitamos el pueblo, comimos en los restaurantes locales y viajamos a Valencia para ver la ciudad. Valencia es una ciudad muy moderna. ¡Me encantó! **Durante las vacaciones** hizo muchísimo calor.

En Buñol se puede participar en la batalla de tomates más grande del mundo: la Tomatina. Las autoridades dicen que el año pasado participaron 40.000 personas. Todos tiramos tomates, muchos tomates, 100 toneladas de tomates que costaron unos 6.000 euros.

La fiesta fue **el último miércoles de agosto** y duró dos horas. ¡Pintaron toda la plaza y las calles de Buñol de rojo, pero nosotros lo pasamos bomba! Me encantó la fiesta porque fue muy divertida.

Lamentablemente **este verano** no puedo volver a Buñol porque no voy a tener suficiente dinero, pero recomiendo la Tomatina a todos.

Martín

 LEER 1 NC 5

¿Qué significan las frases en negrita?
Ejemplo: a finales de agosto – at the end of August

 LEER 2 NC 5

**Lee el texto y contesta a las preguntas en español.
Da respuestas completas.**

1 ¿Adónde fue Martín de vacaciones?
2 ¿Con quién fue?
3 ¿Cómo viajó?
4 ¿Dónde se alojó?
5 ¿Qué tiempo hizo?
6 ¿Qué hizo allí?

 LEER 3 NC 5

¿Verdadero o falso? Corrige las frases falsas.

1 Buñol atrae a muchos turistas.
2 La Tomatina es en julio.
3 No existen batallas de tomates más grandes.
4 Se tiran unos 40.000 tomates.
5 La fiesta dura todo el día.
6 La plaza y las calles terminaron muy sucias.

 ESCRIBIR 4 NC 4–5

Investigación cultural. Busca información sobre otra fiesta española o latinoamericana y diseña un póster en inglés con la información clave.

 See Zoom OxBox

Escuchar

NC 5

Listen, and copy and fill in the table.

	destination	companion(s)	transport	accommodation	weather	activities	opinion
1							
2							
3							
4							

Hablar

NC 5

Choose one of these cards and answer the questions.

Leer

NC 5

Read the text and answer the questions in English.

1 What is Sam's opinion of his usual holidays?
2 What changed last summer?
3 Mention three things you can do in Ibiza.
4 Mention four activities they did.
5 What was the weather like?
6 What was his opinion of the holiday? Why?

¿Adónde fuiste?

¿Con quién?

¿Cómo?

¿Cuándo?

¿Dónde te alojaste?

¿Qué tiempo hizo?

¿Qué hiciste?

¿Cómo lo pasaste? 🙂

¿Adónde fuiste?

¿Con quién?

¿Cómo?

¿Cuándo?

¿Dónde te alojaste?

¿Qué tiempo hizo?

¿Qué hiciste?

¿Cómo lo pasaste?

Normalmente voy de vacaciones a Andalucía con mi familia y las vacaciones son muy aburridas, pero el verano pasado fui a Ibiza, con mis amigos. Fuimos en avión y durante el viaje leí un libro y escuché música. Pasamos una semana allí y nos alojamos en un hotel muy cómodo.

En Ibiza hay mucho que hacer: se puede ir a la discoteca todos los días, se puede ir a la playa y se pueden visitar monumentos famosos. Mis amigos y yo jugamos al voleibol y practicamos vela.

Durante las vacaciones hizo buen tiempo y lo pasamos fenomenal: comimos platos típicos, bebimos sangría y bailamos en las discotecas.

Fueron unas vacaciones muy emocionantes y divertidas y muy diferentes a las vacaciones que paso con mis padres en Andalucía.

Sam

Escribir

NC 5-6

Write an account of a real or imaginary holiday to a Spanish destination. Aim to achieve a Level 5 or above.

See Zoom OxBox

¿Qué se puede hacer?	What can you do?
se puede	you can/you are allowed
no se puede	you can't/you are not allowed
se puede visitar	you can visit
se puede ir	you can go
se puede ver	you can see
se puede pasear	you can go for a walk
se puede pescar	you can fish
se puede comprar	you can shop/buy
se puede jugar	you can play
se puede hacer	you can do
el río	the river
al aire libre	outdoors/outside
lamentablemente	unfortunately

¿Adónde fuiste?	Where did you go?
el verano pasado	last summer
el invierno pasado	last winter
el año pasado	last year
hace dos años	two years ago
el pasado junio	last June
las Navidades pasadas	last Christmas
hizo sol	it was sunny
hizo calor	it was hot
hizo frío	it was cold
hizo viento	it was windy
hizo buen tiempo	the weather was nice
hizo mal tiempo	the weather was bad
estuvo nublado	it was cloudy
hubo tormenta	there was a storm
hubo niebla	it was foggy
llovió	it rained

¿Qué hiciste?	What did you do?
alojarse/nos alojamos	to stay/we stayed (accommodation)
hacer/hice vela	to do/I did sailing
tomar/tomé el sol	to sunbathe/I sunbathed
bañarse/me bañé en el mar	to swim/I swam in the sea
comer/comimos comida típica	to eat/we ate typical food
relajarse/nos relajamos	to relax/we relaxed
pasear/paseamos	to go for a walk/we went for a walk
sacar/saqué muchas fotos	to take/I took lots of photos
salir/salí de compras	to go out/I went out shopping
comprar/compré recuerdos	to buy/I bought souvenirs
escribir/escribí unas postales	to write/I wrote some postcards
la mayoría de las tardes	most evenings
volver/volví a casa	to return/I returned home

¿Lo pasaste bien?	Did you have a good time?
¡Lo pasé/pasamos fenomenal!	I/we had a great time!
¡Lo pasé/pasamos bomba!	I/we had a blast!
¡Qué aburrido!	How boring!
¡Qué desastre!	What a disaster!
fue/fueron regular	it was/they were average
fue/fueron muy emocionante(s)	it was/they were very exciting
fue/fueron increíble(s)	it was/they were incredible
no estuvo/estuvieron mal	it wasn't/they weren't bad
me/nos encantó	I /we loved it
me/nos gustó	I/we liked it

¿Qué compraste?	What did you buy?
un imán	a magnet
unas castañuelas	castanets
un abanico	a (typically Spanish) fan
una camiseta	a t-shirt
un vestido de flamenco	a flamenco dress
una guitarra española	a Spanish guitar
una muñeca	a doll
un sombrero	a hat
un llavero	a key ring
unas gafas de sol	sunglasses
el/la dependiente	shop assistant
el/la cliente	customer
¿Qué deseas?	What would you like?
¿Cuánto cuesta?	How much does it cost?
muy caro/a	very expensive
algo más barato/a	something cheaper
¡Mira!	Look!
Me lo quedo	I'll take it
¿Algo más?	Anything else?

I can ...

- say what you can do in my city
- talk about the weather in the past
- list the activities I did on a past holiday
- give my opinion of a past holiday
- use the preterite tense of regular and some irregular verbs correctly

- Vocabulary: talk about different media-based activities, say what you like to watch on TV and why
- Grammar: words of frequency
- Skills: practise questions and answers with a partner

a
hablo por teléfono

b
navego por internet

c
veo la televisión

d
escucho la radio

e
juego con videojuegos

f
utilizo el correo electrónico

g
leo los periódicos

h
leo revistas

i
participo en los chats

Gramática → p.167

Remember:
hablo por teléfono – **I talk** on the telephone
BUT
me gusta hablar por teléfono – **I like talking** on the telephone

ESCUCHAR 1

 Escucha. ¿Les gustan o no les gustan?
Listen and decide if the people like these activities or not. Write the appropriate letters and ticks/crosses.

Ejemplo: **1** Sara – a ✓ g ✗

1 Sara **2** Miguel **3** Jaime **4** Maite

LEER 2

Lee el correo electrónico de Javi.
Read Javi's email. Copy and complete the sentences.

1 Javi sometimes ▒▒▒ **3** Javi never ▒▒▒
2 Javi often ▒▒▒ **4** Javi ▒▒▒

Hablo por teléfono con mis amigos todos los días. Me gusta utilizar el correo electrónico de vez en cuando – más o menos una vez a la semana. Veo la televisión muy a menudo – ¡me encanta! Nunca leo los periódicos – ¡qué aburrido!

Javi

hablo por teléfono
navego por internet
veo la televisión
escucho la radio
juego con videojuegos
utilizo el correo electrónico
leo los periódicos
leo revistas
participo en los chats
de vez en cuando
todos los días
una vez / tres veces a la semana
nunca
a menudo

 **See Zoom OxBox**

HABLAR 3

NC 3

Juega a las 20 preguntas.
Play 20 questions with your partner. Can you guess what they like doing and how often?

Ejemplo: A ¿Navegas por internet?
      B No.
      A ¿Juegas con videojuegos?
      B Sí.
      A ¿Todos los días?
      B ¡Sí!

los dibujos animados — las series — los anuncios
los programas deportivos — las telenovelas — los concursos
los programas musicales — los documentales — las noticias

ESCUCHAR 4

Escucha. ¿Quién gana?
Listen carefully. Who wins the game of noughts and crosses?

HABLAR 5

NC 3

Juega con tu compañero.
Play noughts and crosses with your partner.

ESCUCHAR 6

Escucha. ¿Qué opinan?
Listen. What do they think?

Ejemplo: 1 Las telenovelas son tontas pero graciosas.

ESCRIBIR 7

NC 4

Escribe. ¿Estás de acuerdo con los otros?
Do you agree with the opinions in Activity 6? Write out what you think.

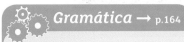

Gramática → p.164

Remember:

hablo – I speak
hablas – you speak
leo – I read
lees – you read

Which verbs follow the same pattern?

Veo la televisión todo el día.

? Think

El programa does not follow the usual pattern – it is a masculine word, but ends in *a*. Can you find any other words like it?

divertido/a   emocionante
gracioso/a   informativo/a
tonto/a

Challenge
Write about the activities you do. Which ones do you do? How often do you do them? Which TV programmes do you like to watch? Which ones don't you like? Why? Include as much information as you can and word-process your statement. Can your friends guess who you are? NC 4

- Vocabulary: talk about the type of films you like and why
- Grammar: practise using *gustar* to say what other people like
- Skills: carry out a survey

HABLAR 1 👥 **Habla con tu compañero.**

Discuss with your partner what the different types of films are.
What helped you decide?

ESCUCHAR 2 🎧 **Escucha y lee. ¡No es correcto!**

Listen and read. Find the errors in the sentences.

*Ejemplo: 1 Me encantan las películas de ~~terror~~ (acción) –
¡son emocionantes!*

1 Me encantan las películas de terror – ¡son emocionantes!
2 En mi opinión, las películas de guerra son tontas.
   No me gustan.
3 Las comedias son interesantes. Son mi tipo de películas
   preferidas.
4 Para mí, las películas de ciencia-ficción son aburridas.
   Las veo a menudo.
5 No me gustan nada las películas románticas. Son graciosas.
6 Las películas de vaqueros son divertidas. Pero me
   gustan mucho.

> una película romántica
> una película de terror
> una película de ciencia-ficción
> una película de vaqueros
> una película de acción
> una película de misterio
> una película de guerra
> una comedia

ESCUCHAR 3 🎧 **Escucha otra vez. Escribe las frases correctamente.**

Listen again if necessary. Write the sentences out correctly.

Ejemplo: Me encantan las películas de acción – ¡son emocionantes!

See Zoom OxBox

Habla con tu compañero. ¿Qué tipo de películas no le gustan a Eva?

What type of films do you think Eva does not like?

 Mira el video.

Watch the video. What are they talking about? What does Eva want Marisa to do? What does Marisa want Eva to do?

1	*¿Te gusta leer libros?*
2	*¿Por qué?*
3	*¿Leiste un libro la semana pasada?*
4	*¿Leiste un libro el mes pasado?*
5	*¿Leiste un libro el año pasado?*
6	*¿Qué prefieres hacer? ¿Por qué?*
7	*Da el título de un libro que conoces.*
8	*¿Qué tipo de libro es?*

 Escucha a Tomás. ¿Cómo responde a las preguntas?

Listen to Tomás. How does he answer the questions?

*Ejemplo: **1** De vez en cuando*

 Habla con tus compañeros. ¿Qué dicen?

Do the survey with your friends. What do they say?

NC 4–5

 Escribe sus respuestas.

Write down their answers.

NC 4–5

Ejemplo: 20 personas piensan que los libros son aburridos.

⚙ *Gramática* → p.167

To say 'somebody likes ...' put *a* in front of the person's name, followed by *le gusta*:
***A** Tomás le gusta leer libros de vez en cuando.*

Remember:

me gusta – I like (it)	*nos gusta* – we like (it)
te gusta – you like (it)	*os gusta* – you (pl) like (it)
le gusta – he / she likes (it)	*les gusta* – they like (it)

Challenge

Advertise your favourite film for the local Spanish film club.

NC 4–5

 **See Zoom OxBox**

4B.3 ¿De qué trató? ¿Qué pasó?

- Vocabulary: describe what a film is about and what happened
- Grammar: practise using the preterite tense
- Skills: look up verbs in a dictionary

¿Qué hiciste el sábado?

Fui al cine para ver una película.

¿De qué trató?

Empareja los dibujos y las palabras.
Work with a partner to match up the pictures of the films and their descriptions.

Ejemplo: **a** *un atentado*

Escucha. ¿De qué trató la película?
What was the film about?

Ejemplo: **1** *Trató de una guerra. – k*

Habla con tu compañero.
Which film are you thinking of? How quickly can your partner guess?

NC 2–3

Ejemplo: **A** *¿Trató de una amistad?*
B *No.*
A *¿Trató de un robo?*
B *Sí.*
A *Es la letra g.*

---

trató de
un asesinato
un atentado
un robo
un secuestro
un timo
un viaje
una amistad
una guerra
una historia de amor
una lucha entre el bien y el mal
una misión secreta
vampiros

? Think

Remember cognates – words that look similar in Spanish and English.

¿Qué pasó?			
	un astronauta	buscó	un casino
	un espía	batallaron contra	el novio de su amiga
	una estudiante	robaron	los ángeles
	unos ladrones	descubrió	un asesinato misterioso
	unos vampiros	solucionó	una bomba atómica
	un policía	se enamoró de	un planeta nuevo

LEER 4 👥 **¿Qué pasó? Haz frases correctas.**
Work with a partner to find the correct descriptions.

Ejemplo: Un astronauta descubrió un planeta nuevo.

ESCUCHAR 5 🎧 **Escucha. ¿Tienes razón?**
Listen. Were you right?

VIDEO 6 🎥 **Mira el video.**
Watch the video. What are Eva and Marisa talking about?
What happens in their story?

 **Challenge**
Write a brief film review and present it to the class. Remember to include the title, the type of film, what it was about, what happened and what your opinion was.

NC 4–6

 *Gramática* → p.164

Looking up verbs
If you want to know what *descubrió* means, you will need to look up its infinitive form, *descubrir*, in the dictionary.

Descubrir means 'to discover', so *descubrió* means 'he or she discovered'.

If you don't know what the infinitive form is, you know it has to end in -*ar*, -*er* or -*ir*. Look in the dictionary for a word which starts like the one you want to know, and has one of those endings.

If this doesn't work, you may be looking up an irregular verb. Try the verb tables in a dictionary.

 See Zoom OxBox

4B.4 Repaso

- Vocabulary: revise what you have learnt so far
- Grammar: ask and answer questions
- Skills: independent learning

HABLAR 1 · NC 4–5

 Entrevista a tu compañero.

Interview a friend. Prepare to answer these questions.
Act out your interview to the class.

Info personal

¿Cómo te llamas?
¿Cuántos años tienes?
¿Cuántas personas hay en tu familia?
¿Cuándo es tu cumpleaños?
¿De qué nacionalidad eres?
¿Cómo eres?

El insti

¿Cómo es tu instituto?
¿Cuál es tu asignatura preferida?
¿Tienes uniforme?

Tu vida

¿Qué te gusta hacer en tu tiempo libre?
¿Cómo es tu rutina diaria?
¿Dónde vives?
¿Cómo es tu casa?
¿Cómo es tu dormitorio?
¿Qué te gusta comer?

Tus vacaciones

¿Adónde vas de vacaciones?
¿Qué haces cuando estás de vacaciones?
¿Qué hiciste durante las vacaciones del año pasado?

Los medios

¿Cómo comunicas con tus amigos – por móvil, correo electrónico, SMS?
¿Qué te gusta ver en la televisión?
¿Cuál fue la última película que viste? ¿De qué trató?

ESCRIBIR 2 · NC 4–5

 Describe una persona.

Write a description of one of these people.

- What are they called?
- How old are they?
- Where do they live?
- What's their family like?
- What do they like doing?
- What do they think of school?

Use the questions above to help you, and look back through the book for any information you need.

 **See Zoom OxBox**

Encuesta

🎧 **Escuchar**

 **a**  **b**  **c**

1 ¿Quién es?

14 **14** **15**

2 Melisa vive en
  a una ciudad en el norte de España.
  b una ciudad en el sur de España.
  c un pueblo en el sur de España.

3 En el instituto, Miguel prefiere
  a la historia
  b el inglés
  c la tecnología
    porque es
  d bastante divertida.
  e muy interesante.
  f bastante fácil.

4 Pon en orden:

Desayuno
Me despierto
Me ducho
Me levanto
Me peino
Me pongo el
  uniforme

Leer y escribir

NC 4–5

1 ¿A qué hora? Copia y completa las frases sobre ti.
  a Tomo el desayuno a _____ de la mañana / tarde.
  b Tomo la comida a _____ de la mañana / tarde.
  c Tomo la cena a _____ de la mañana / tarde.

2 Vacaciones maravillosas. ¿Qué vas a hacer?
Copia y completa.

Este verano (ir – nosotros) *vamos* a ir de vacaciones.
(alojarse – nosotros) _____ en un hotel muy grande.
(hacer – yo) _____ el surf, pero mi hermana (tomar el sol – ella)
_____ . Mis padres (comer – ellos) _____ tapas en el bar.
Y tú, ¿qué (hacer – tú) _____ ?

3 ¿Qué se puede hacer donde vives? ¿Por qué? Escribe tres frases.

4 Copia y corrige las frases.
  a No me gusta las telenovelas – son tontos.
  b Me encantan ver las anuncios – normalmente son graciosos.
  c Me gusta los programas deportivas. Es emocionantes.
  d No me gusta nada las documentales – es aburrido.

- Vocabulary: describe the advantages and disadvantages of different types of media
- Grammar: use *lo bueno* and *lo malo*
- Skills: present and defend a point of view

11. leer libros

1. hablar por teléfono

10. ir al cine

2. navegar por internet

9. participar en los chats

3. ver la televisión

8. leer revistas

4. escuchar la radio

7. leer los periódicos

6. utilizar el correo electrónico

5. jugar con videojuegos

k. peligroso
j. fácil
i. entretenido
h. educativo
g. gracioso

a. divertido
b. útil
c. rápido
d. personal
e. emocionante

f. tonto

HABLAR 1

NC 2–3

¿Qué opinas?
What do you think? Match the adjectives to the types of activity.

Ejemplo: Jugar con videojuegos es muy emocionante.

HABLAR 2

¡Al contrario!
What **aren't** these activities? Make some negative statements.

Ejemplo: Leer libros no es muy divertido.

ESCUCHAR 3

🎧 **Escucha. ¿Qué opinan?**
What do Beatriz and Alfonso think? Copy and complete the table.

Actividad	Beatriz	Alfonso

es muy ...	emocionante
no es muy ...	tonto
puede ser ...	gracioso
divertido	educativo
útil	entretenido
rápido	fácil
personal	peligroso

⚙ Gramática

Lo bueno es que ... – The good thing is that ...
Lo bueno de ... es que ... – The good thing about ... is that ...

How would you talk about bad things?

See Zoom OxBox

HABLAR 4

NC 3–4

¿Una ventaja o una desventaja?
Would you describe the following as an advantage or disadvantage to the different activities?

Ejemplo: 1 Es una pérdida de tiempo – una desventaja

? Think

Se puede hacer en casa, en el parque, en el tren, en el instituto – ¡se puede hacer donde quieras!

What does *donde quieras* mean?

1  Es una pérdida de tiempo.

2 Se puede hacer con amigos.

3 Se puede hacer solo.

4 Se puede hacer en casa.

5 Se puede llevar adonde quieras.

6 Necesitas tecnología especial.

7 Es caro.

8 Es antisocial.

ESCUCHAR 5

🎧 **Escucha. Nota las ventajas y las desventajas.**
Listen and note the advantages and disadvantages of these activities.

1  **2** **3**  **4**

HABLAR 6

NC 3–4

👥 **Encuentra un compañero.**
Find someone else who thinks the same thing as you.

Ejemplo: **A** *Creo que navegar por internet es antisocial.*
B *No estoy de acuerdo. Lo bueno es que se puede hacer solo.*

una ventaja es ...
una desventaja es ...
lo malo es que ...
lo bueno es que ...
es una pérdida de tiempo
se puede hacer ... con amigos / solo
  / en casa / donde quieras
se puede llevar consigo / adonde
  quieras
(no) necesitas tecnología especial
(no) es caro
es antisocial

Challenge

Hold a debate. Work with a group to present an argument for or against a particular activity.

NC 4–5

⟐ **See Zoom OxBox**

Comprender – Verbs and opinions

A *Ayer, hoy y mañana*

Putting it all together! Here's how you talk about what you **do**, what you **did** and what you are **going to do**.

Normalmente desayuno a las siete. Ayer desayuné a las siete y cuarto. Mañana es sábado – ¡voy a desayunar a las diez!

Normally I eat breakfast at 7 o'clock. Yesterday I ate breakfast at a quarter past seven. Tomorrow is Saturday – I'm going to eat breakfast at 10 o'clock!

Normally / today – present tense
Yesterday / last week – preterite tense
Tomorrow / next week – immediate future tense

1 **Copy and complete these sentences. Use the words in the box.**

Normalmente (**1**) _____ al instituto. Ayer (**2**) _____ al cine. Mañana (**3**) _____ a la playa.

Normalmente (**4**) _____ un bocadillo en el comedor del instituto. Ayer (**5**) _____ patatas fritas con mis amigos. Mañana (**6**) _____ en un restaurante con mi familia.

> como   voy a ir   fui
> voy a comer   comí   voy

2 **Write sentences about what you normally do, did yesterday and are going to do tomorrow using activities from this unit.**

Example: Normalmente escucho la radio. Ayer hablé por teléfono. Mañana voy a navegar por internet.

> hoy   normalmente
> ayer   la semana pasada
> mañana   la semana que viene

B *Lo bueno y lo malo* – expressing opinions

lo bueno es que ... – a/the good thing is that ...

lo malo es que ... – a/the bad thing is that ...

Me gusta ver las telenovelas. Lo bueno es que son divertidas. Lo malo es que son tontas.

I like watching TV soaps. The good thing is that they're fun. The bad thing is that they're silly.

3 **Complete these sentences. Use the words below.**

1 Me gusta navegar por _____ . Lo bueno es que es _____ . Lo malo es que es _____ .

2 No me gusta mucho leer _____ . Lo malo es que es _____ . Lo bueno es que se puede _____ consigo.

> aburrido   educativo   antisocial   internet   libros   llevar

4 **What is the good thing or the bad thing about:**

- using chat rooms
- going to the cinema
- reading books
- using email?t

lo bueno de ... es que ... – the good thing **about** ... is that ...

lo malo de ... es que ... – the bad thing **about** ... is that ...

Aprender – Irregular verbs

C Remembering irregular verbs

Sometimes it can seem that there are a lot of verbs to remember. But when you are using the preterite (past) tense, for most verbs you only need to remember the first person (**I** did something) and the rest follows a pattern.

poner = to put
*Ayer **puse** la revista en la televisión.* = Yesterday **I put** the magazine on the TV.

Poner is an *-er* verb, and uses the same endings you have learnt for other irregular verbs like *tener* and *hacer*. They are very similar to the regular endings for *-er* verbs.

Look at the box on the right. Where are the endings different?
How many different endings do you actually have to learn?

How would you say 'you put the magazine on the TV yesterday'?

poder = to be able (I can, I could)
It follows the same pattern as *poner*.
*No **pude** ir al instituto ayer.* – **I couldn't** go to school yesterday.
How would you say:
'He couldn't go to school yesterday'
'We couldn't go to school yesterday'?

poner	comer
puse	comí
pusiste	comiste
puso	comió
pusimos	comimos
pusisteis	comisteis
pusieron	comieron

Here are the first person (I) preterite forms for some useful irregular verbs.

navegar – navegué
jugar – jugué
ver – vi
leer – leí

Hablar – Asking questions

D Communicating with questions

It's difficult to communicate with someone without asking questions.

5 🎧 **Listen to these people. Are they asking a question or making a statement?**

6 **Make up questions that go with these statements; look back through the book to help you.**

1 Me llamo Raúl.
2 Tengo doce años.
3 Hay cinco personas en mi familia.
4 Vivo en Barcelona.
5 Me gusta ver los programas deportivos.

7 🎧 **Now listen – were you right?**

8 👥 **Practise the questions from Activity 6 with a partner – they read out the statement, you say the correct question. Does it sound like a question when you say it?**

▶ **See Zoom OxBox**

- Vocabulary: understand which TV programmes other people like
- Grammar: practise using *me gusta* and *me gusta ver*
- Skills: personalise a template

Veo la televisión todos los días. ¡Me gusta mucho! Me interesan bastante las noticias – son importantes, pero prefiero los programas deportivos, sobre todo de fútbol. También me gustan las telenovelas – ¡son graciosas! No me gustan nada los documentales. Y los concursos – ¡ni hablar! ¡Qué tontería!

No veo mucho la televisión, pero me gustan los programas de música. Quiero decir, los programas de música clásica o música catalana tradicional, claro. También me interesan los documentales sobre arte o literatura. En mi opinión, las telenovelas son tontas y los concursos son ridículos.

LEER 1

NC 3–4

¿Verdad o mentira?

Are these statements true or false?

1 A Eva le gustan los programas de música.
2 Eva piensa que los documentales son tontos.
3 A Eva no le gustan los concursos.
4 Marisa ve la televisión dos veces a la semana.
5 A Marisa le gustan los programas de fútbol.
6 Marisa piensa que los concursos son una tontería.

una tontería

VIDEO 2

NC 3

📹 Mira el video-blog.

What type of films do they like? What do they like watching on TV? Why?

ESCRIBIR 3

NC 2–3

Describe lo que te gusta ver en la televisión.

Describe what you like watching on TV. Copy and complete.

Normalmente veo la televisión ▨▨▨ veces a la semana.

Me gustan los programas de ▨▨▨ porque son ▨▨▨ . También

me gusta ver ▨▨▨ – en mi opinión son ▨▨▨ . No me gustan

nada los programas de ▨▨▨ – son ▨▨▨ . Mi programa favorito

se llama ▨▨▨ . Trata de ▨▨▨ . Me gusta porque es ▨▨▨ .

⚙ *Gramática* → p.167

Remember:

Me gusta la televisión – singular

Me gustan los programas deportivos – plural

Me gusta ver la televisión – I like + verb = I like **doing** something

See Zoom OxBox

- Vocabulary: talk about films
- Grammar: practise recognising and using verbs
- Skills: write a description

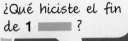

¿Qué hiciste el fin de 1 _____ ?

Fui al 2 _____ .
Vi la nueva película de Harry Potter.

¿Harry Potter? ¿Qué tipo de 3 _____ es?

¿Cómo? ¿No conoces a Harry Potter? ¡Es muy 4 _____ ! Es una película de 5 _____ .

Pues, no me 6 _____ las películas de fantasía. Son 7 _____ .

No, no – ¡es 8 _____ emocionante! Trata de un chico, Harry, que es mago, y de todas sus 9 _____ en el colegio de magos.

Mm, no sé ... Una película que 10 _____ de un colegio ...

Tienes que verla. ¡Es genial!

 1 Completa la historia. Usa las palabras de la casilla.

NC 4–5

 2 Escucha. ¿Tienes razón?

NC 4

 3 Explica lo que pasó. ¿Qué hizo el chico? ¿Qué piensa? ¿Qué piensa la chica? ¿De qué trató la película?

NC 4–5

 4 Busca los verbos. ¿Son en presente o pasado? Escribe los infinitivos.

 5 Describe una película. ¿Qué tipo de película es? ¿De qué trata? ¿Qué piensas?

NC 4–6

aventuras	muy
cine	película
famoso	semana
fantasía	tontas
gustan	trata

? Think

How do you say:

It's about ...
Don't you know about ... ?
You have to see it!

 See Zoom OxBox

Escuchar

NC 3–4

Which TV programmes are they talking about?
What do they think of them?

a **b** **c** **d** **e** **f**

 Hablar

NC 3–4

Describe what you do in your free time and how often you do it.

 Leer

NC 4–5

Match the reviews to the pictures.

1  **2**  **3**

a Una película muy emocionante. Trata de un asesinato. Un policía quiere solucionar la muerte de una persona muy famosa.

b Una película inteligente y graciosa. Dos amigos descubren un robo. Pero, ¿trata de ladrones o espías? Ése es el misterio.

 Escribir

NC 4–6

Describe a film. Include what type of film it is, what it was about, and what happened. What do you think of it?

c Es una película que trata de una misión secreta en el futuro. Pero el espía se enamora de la hija de su enemigo.

See Zoom OxBox

Los medios y la televisión — The media and television

hablo por teléfono	I talk on the phone
navego por internet	I surf the net
veo la televisión	I watch TV
escucho la radio	I listen to the radio
juego con videojuegos	I play computer games
utilizo el correo electrónico	I email
leo los periódicos	I read the newspapers
leo revistas	I read magazines
participo en los chats	I use chatrooms
de vez en cuando	sometimes
todos los días	every day
una vez / tres veces a la semana	once / three times a week
nunca	never
a menudo	often
divertido/a	entertaining
gracioso/a	funny
tonto/a	stupid
emocionante	exciting
informativo/a	informative
las noticias	news
las series	series
las telenovelas	TV soaps
los anuncios	adverts
los concursos	game shows
los dibujos animados	cartoons
los documentales	documentaries
los programas deportivos	sports programmes
los programas musicales	music programmes

El cine y los libros — Cinema and books

una película romántica	a romantic film
una película de terror	a horror film
una película de ciencia-ficción	a sci-fi film
una película de vaqueros	a cowboy film
una película de acción	an action film
una película de misterio	a mystery film
una película de guerra	a war film
una comedia	a comedy
la fantasía	fantasy

¿De qué trató? ¿Qué pasó? — What was it about? What happened?

un asesinato	a murder
un atentado	a terrorist attack
un robo	a robbery
un secuestro	a kidnap
un timo	a scam
un viaje	a journey
una amistad	a friendship
una guerra	a war
una historia de amor	a love story

una lucha entre el bien y el mal	a struggle between good and evil
una misión secreta	a secret mission
vampiros	vampires
buscar	to look for
batallar	to fight
robar	to rob
descubrir	to find
solucionar	to solve
enamorarse de	to fall in love with

En mi opinión ... — In my opinion ...

es muy ...	it's very ...
puede ser ...	it can be ...
útil	useful
rápido/a	quick
personal	personal
educativo/a	educational
entretenido/a	entertaining
fácil	easy
peligroso/a	dangerous
una ventaja es ...	an advantage is ...
una desventaja es ...	a disadvantage is ...
lo malo es que ...	the bad thing is ...
lo bueno es que ...	the good thing is ...
es una pérdida de tiempo	it's a waste of time
se puede hacer ...	you can do it ...
con amigos / solo / en casa / donde quieras	with friends / alone / at home / wherever you like
se puede llevar consigo / adonde quieras	you can take it with you / wherever you like
(no) necesitas tecnología especial	you (don't) need special technology
(no) es caro/a	it's (not) expensive

Extra — Extra

una tontería	a stupid thing
tienes que verlo	you have to see it
¿No conoces ...?	Don't you know ...?

◎ I can ...

- ◉ talk about different media-based activities, say what I like to watch on TV and why
- ◉ talk about the type of films I like and why
- ◉ describe what a film is about and what happened
- ◉ describe the advantages and disadvantages of different media

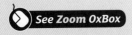 See Zoom OxBox

Ley del Registro Civil

Art. 8.º En el Libro de Familia se certificará a todos los efectos, gratuitamente, de los hechos y circunstancias que determine el Reglamento, inmediatamente de la inscripción de los mismos.

Reglamento del Registro Civil

Art. 36. El Libro de Familia se abre con la certificación del matrimonio no secreto y contiene sucesivas hojas destinadas a certificar las indicaciones registrales sobre el régimen económico de la sociedad conyugal, el nacimiento de los hijos comunes y de los adoptados conjuntamente por ambos contrayentes, el fallecimiento de los cónyuges y la nulidad, divorcio o separación del matrimonio.—También se entregará Libro de Familia al progenitor o progenitores de un hijo no matrimonial y a la persona o personas que adopten a un menor. Se hará constar, en su caso, el matrimonio que posteriormente contraigan entre sí los titulares del Libro.—En el Libro se asentará con valor de certificación cualquier hecho que afecte a la patria potestad y la defunción de los hijos, si ocurre antes de la emancipación.—Los asientos-certificaciones son en extracto sin transcripción de notas, y en los de nacimiento no se expresará la clase de filiación. Pueden rectificarse en virtud de ulterior asiento-certificación.

Art. 37. El Libro de Familia se entregará a sus titulares, o a personas autorizadas por éstos, inmediatamente después de la inscripción del matrimonio en el Registro ordinario o, salvo que ya lo tuvieren, cuando se inscriba una filiación no matrimonial o una adopción.—Cuando la entrega del Libro tenga lugar por consecuencia de la inscripción de una adopción, habrá de cancelarse el asiento de nacimiento que figure en el anterior Libro de Familia expedido, en su caso, al progenitor o progenitores por naturaleza. Si en este Libro anterior consta únicamente ese asiento de nacimiento dicho Libro será anulado.

Art. 38. La entrega del Libro, cualquiera que sea el tiempo en que tenga lugar, se hará constar siempre al margen de la correspondiente inscripción de matrimonio o, en defecto de éste, en cada una de las inscripciones de nacimiento.—Los cónyuges o el titular o titulares de la patria potestad tendrán siempre el Libro correspondiente. En caso de pérdida o deterioro, obtendrán del mismo Registro un duplicado en el que se extenderán las certificaciones oportunas. En el duplicado se expresará que sustituye al primitivo y de su expedición se tomará nota en las inscripciones correspondientes del Registro.

0003254

MINISTERIO DE JUSTICIA
DIRECCIÓN GENERAL DE LOS REGISTROS Y DEL NOTARIADO

LIBRO DE FAMILIA

EXPEDIDO PARA

D. *Carlos José Guerra y Sanz*

y D.ª *Oretta Lambagha y Ramírez*

(Si sólo hay un titular, déjese en blanco el espacio correspondiente.)

(No serán considerados ejemplares editados oficialmente los que no lleven el sello en seco del Ministerio de Justicia.)

Modelo oficial aprobado por Orden ministerial de 20 de julio de 1989 («BOE» de 13 de septiembre de 1989)

EDICIÓN 1999
EJEMPLAR GRATUITO
(Ley 25/1986, de 24 de diciembre)

> Todas las familias en España tienen un Libro de Familia. Es un documento oficial en que se registran los nombres de los hijos. Todos los hijos tienen un Documento Nacional de Identidad o DNI. El Libro también se usa para la Seguridad Social, cuando se casa o se divorcia y cuando se muere.

LEER 1

Explain in your own words what the *Libro de Familia* is. Do you think this is a good idea?

> Hola, me llamo Amira. Tengo 36 años. Soy de Barranquilla en Colombia.

> Saludos de Tenerife en las Islas Canarias. Soy Jorge Buitrago y tengo dieciséis años.

> Buenas tardes de Santiago, la capital de Chile. Me llamo Juan Carlos y tengo cincuenta y dos años.

> Buenos días; me llamo Carmiña y soy de Cuzco en Perú. Tengo veintidós años.

LEER 2

Answer the questions.

1 Who is from Colombia?
2 How old is Carmiña?
3 Where does Juan Carlos come from?
4 Who is sixteen?
5 Where is Cuzco?

See Zoom OxBox

Yo soy Bea, la fea

Ugly Betty no es una serie original americana, es una adaptación de una telenovela colombiana fantástica y muy famosa en Colombia y el resto de los países de Sudamérica. *Yo soy Bea, la fea* es el título original de la famosa serie colombiana traducida a quince idiomas diferentes y con unas veintidós adaptaciones.

Alemanes, belgas, chinos, españoles, franceses, griegos, indios, israelís, rusos, turcos e incluso vietnamitas pueden ver *Yo soy Bea, la fea* en sus televisiones.

En la serie, Bea es secretaria y es delgada y de talla mediana. Tiene los ojos negros, el pelo largo y negro y lleva gafas pero no es muy atractiva. Sin embargo, Bea es muy estudiosa, responsable, muy inteligente y brillante.

En el 2010, después de haber sido emitida en más de 100 países, *Yo soy Bea, la fea* entró en el libro de los Guinness World Records.

 1 **Read and choose the correct answer.**

1 *Ugly Betty* is
  a an original American sitcom.
  b an adaptation of a famous Colombian sitcom.

2 *Yo soy Bea, la fea*
  a has been translated into 15 different languages.
  b exists in 15 countries.

3 Amongst other countries, *Yo soy Bea, la fea* is watched in
  a Russia, Saudi Arabia, France and Greece.
  b Vietnam, China, Belgium and Turkey.

4 In the Colombian sitcom Betty is
  a short and fat.
  b slim and average height.

5 *Yo soy Bea, la fea* has entered the Guinness Book of World Records after
  a it was aired in over 100 countries.
  b it aired its 100th episode.

 2 **Read again and find the following:**
  ● 10 countries that watch *Ugly Betty*
  ● 5 physical attributes of Bea
  ● 4 personality attributes

 NC 4 **Your turn! Describe your favourite character from a soap opera, cartoon or sitcom.**

Mi instituto es el Instituto Lope de Vega de Madrid. Es un instituto muy grande en el centro de la capital de España. El instituto es viejo, pero las aulas son modernas. Me gusta mucho mi instituto – ¡tengo muchos amigos!

Beatriz

El Instituto Rafael Arozarena es un instituto bastante grande y moderno en la isla de Tenerife. Hay clases desde las ocho de la mañana hasta las dos de la tarde. Me encanta mi instituto porque charlo con mis amigos.

Rodrigo

Mi instituto se llama El Minuto de Dios en Bogotá, Colombia. Es bastante pequeño. Me encanta mi instituto – mi familia no tiene mucho dinero y tener una educación es muy importante en Bogotá.

Iván

Mi instituto es muy pequeño. Sólo tenemos una aula y cuarenta estudiantes. Es el instituto Elementario de las islas flotantes en el Lago Titicaca de Perú. Me gusta mucho mi instituto – quiero tener una buena educación.

Delia

LEER 1 Match the school descriptions to the photos.

LEER 2 Who ...
1 goes to school at 8 a.m.?
2 goes to school in the capital city of Spain?
3 lives on an island?
4 doesn't have much money in their family?
5 thinks education is very important?
6 goes to a modern school in an old building?

LEER 3 What is amazing about the Peruvian islands mentioned?

LEER 4 Why do you think the students in Madrid and Tenerife mention friends, but those from Colombia and Peru talk about education?

See Zoom OxBox

El Calendario Tiempo Libre

Si te interesa el fútbol puedes seguir La Liga con equipos como el Barça o el Real Madrid que dominan todo el año, y en junio está La Copa del Rey que es un trofeo nacional.

Si prefieres el tenis puedes ver a Rafa Nadal, entre muchos otros tenistas españoles e internacionales, en el Trofeo Conde de Godó en abril, en Barcelona.

En mayo, si te entusiasma el deporte de las carreras, puedes ver a uno de los campeones de Fórmula Uno, Fernando Alonso, en el circuito de Monmeló también en Barcelona. En cambio, si prefieres las carreras sobre dos ruedas, el Gran Prix de motociclismo de Jerez de la Frontera se celebra ese mismo mes.

Para los golfistas, hay muchos campos de primera calidad en la Costa del Sol donde celebran el Volvo Masters a finales de octubre.

En Madrid, del ocho al quince de mayo, todos los días hay corridas de toros, en Las Ventas, en honor a San Isidro, el santo patrón de la capital.

La pelota vasca o Jai Alai es un deporte muy antiguo que se juega en el País Vasco. La pelota va muy rápido, puede llegar hasta 220 km/h.

Si te apasiona la música pop, entonces puedes ir a Benicassim para el Festival Internacional de finales de junio.

En cambio, si te fascina el cine y quieres ver a estrellas famosas, entonces tienes que ir a San Sebastián las últimas dos semanas de septiembre para el Festival Internacional Donostia, o a Huelva a finales de noviembre para el Festival del Cine Latinoamericano.

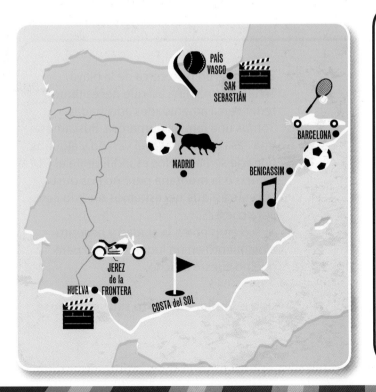

LEER 1 — Read and find the Spanish for:

1 team
2 cycling
3 tennis player
4 circuit
5 champions
6 trophy

LEER 2 — Read and work out:

1 which teams are top of the Spanish League
2 when the Spanish Motorcycle Grand Prix is
3 where the famous golf tournament takes place
4 what happens in Benicassim and when
5 when the two film festivals happen
6 two important facts about *pelota vasca*

☼ Doncasa | En venta

Casa de campo: Riopar, Albacete, €320 000

Vistas de las montañas. Casa ideal para vacaciones. Seis dormitorios y dos cuartos de baño. Cocina completa, calefacción de gas y muebles incluidos. Restaurante cerca.

Piso con balcón: La Herradura, Granada, €225 000

Apartamento increíble con balcón espacioso y vistas a la costa. Situado en la urbanización Cármenes en la reserva natural de Cerro Gordo. Dos dormitorios, dos cuartos de baño y salón espacioso. Cocina completa, aire acondicionado y calefacción central.

Amenidades locales: colegio, playa y parque. Cerca de las tiendas, bares y restaurantes.

Apartamento centro ciudad: Ayamonte, Huelva, €120 000

Apartamento totalmente amueblado. 42 metros cuadrados. 1 dormitorio, salón, cocina y comedor.

Chalet con vistas espectaculares. Gandesa, Tarragona, €299 500

Bonito chalet con vistas al campo. Situado a cuatro kilómetros de la aldea. Incluye cuatro dormitorios y tres cuartos de baño en dos pisos separados que se pueden convertir en uno si se desea. Cocina moderna y salón espacioso con terraza. El jardín está bien cuidado y tiene una piscina de 8m x 4m. Electricidad a través de paneles solares.

LEER 1

Read the adverts. How do you say the following?

1. central heating
2. air conditioning
3. views of the mountains
4. furniture included
5. local facilities

LEER 2

Which house would you recommend to these people?

1. En mi familia somos cuatro: mi madre, mis dos hermanos y yo. Buscamos una casa con jardín y me encantaría tener piscina. Queremos vivir en el campo pero cerca de un pueblo.

2. Buscamos un piso cerca de la playa. Tenemos una niña así que necesitamos tener cerca amenidades adecuadas.

3. Somos una familia numerosa. Buscamos una casa donde pasar el verano y algunos fines de semana. Nos es indiferente el campo o la montaña pero no nos gusta cocinar, así que necesitamos un sitio cerca para comer.

4. Busco empleo en la ciudad y necesito alojamiento en un lugar céntrico pero que no cueste mucho.

ESCRIBIR 3

Design a similar advert to sell your house.

NC 4

⊙ See Zoom OxBox

Madrid y Castilla la Mancha

Queso manchego
Contiene leche de oveja.
Es un queso muy duro y seco.
Se come antes de la comida como entremés.

⤝⤜

Galicia

Pulpo a la feira
Contiene pulpo y patatas,
sal y aceite de oliva.
Es un plato típico de la región.

⤝⤜

Andalucía

Albóndigas
Contienen carne, y se comen
con salsa de tomate.
Se comen como una tapa
o una comida.

⤝⤜

Cataluña

Sarsuela
Contiene diferentes tipos de
pescado y arroz.
Es muy sabrosa. Se come en
la cena o la comida.

País Vasco

Marmitako
Contiene atún, patatas, cebolla, tomates.
Se come en la cena o la comida.

⤝⤜

Valencia

Paella
La comida más famosa de España.
Contiene arroz, pollo, mariscos, gambas y
verduras. Es muy sabrosa.

⤝⤜

Islas Canarias

Papas arrugadas
Contiene patatas cocinadas
con mucha sal.
Se come con carne en la
comida o la cena.

---

aceituna cebolla cocinado duro oveja
pulpo seco sal

LEER 1

True or false? Use the text to help you.

1 Octopus is very popular in Galicia.
2 The most famous dish in all Spain comes from the Canary Islands.
3 *Sarsuela* is made of rice and lots of different fish.
4 You can eat meatballs as a main course or as *tapas*.

5 Manchego cheese is very soft.
6 *Papas arrugadas* is a sweet dessert.
7 Paella is made of both chicken and shellfish.

What other regions of Spain are there? Can you find out about the food that is typical there?

Los Paradores de España

PARADORES

La palabra **parador** significa un lugar donde pararse, hospedarse o alojarse.

Turismo cultural en un alojamiento maravilloso.

- Castillos medievales
- Monasterios o conventos antiguos
- Alcazares moriscos
- Casas de campo antiguas
- Lugares históricos
- Hoteles modernos de primera categoría

El rey Alfonso XIII estableció el sistema de paradores en 1928 para invitar a turistas extranjeros a conocer al país de España. Además quería animar a los españoles a viajar por su tierra y conocer la belleza y variedad de su geografía y sus culturas.

Hoy cuenta con noventa y tres alojamientos modernos y antiguos; unos situados en Parques Nacionales donde puedes disfrutar de la naturaleza; otros situados en lugares de interés histórico o con paisajes increíbles.

Aiguablava – Costa Brava

A unos 46 kilómetros de Girona y 146 de Barcelona este parador moderno de cuatro estrellas se sitúa en un promontorio rocoso de la Costa Brava. Desde aquí puedes visitar el museo y la casa de Gala Dalí en Pubol o el museo Dalí en Girona o Figueres.

En contraste:

Carmona – Sevilla

Otro parador de cuatro estrellas es el Hotel Alcazar del Rey Don Pedro que data del siglo XIV.

LEER 1 Read the text. Using all the reading strategies you have developed, try your best to work out the meanings of new words. Look up words you don't know in a bilingual dictionary. Remind yourself about how to use a dictionary on page 115 first.

LEER 2 What does the word *parador* mean? Do we have anything similar in the UK?

LEER 3 When were the *paradores* established, by whom and for what reason?

LEER 4 Name three different types of *parador*.

⟨⟩ *See Zoom OxBox*

MIS ÚLTIMAS VACACIONES

Before looking at the text below, read these sentences and choose the option that makes most sense for each one.

1 Normalmente voy de vacaciones a ...
  a casa
  b la costa
  c las tres menos cuarto

2 pero el año pasado fui a Bolivia en ...
  a comida típica
  b avión
  c Perú

3 y durante las vacaciones hizo ...
  a mucho calor
  b música
  c a las dos

4 Fui con ...
  a coche
  b recuerdos
  c mis padres

5 y nos alojamos en ...
  a tren
  b un albergue
  c mis amigos

6 En la región se pueden ...
  a hacer muchas actividades
  b sacamos fotos
  c fenomenal

7 Durante las vacaciones ...
  a comer comida típica
  b saqué muchas fotos
  c hace calor

8 y también compré ...
  a museos
  b mis padres
  c recuerdos para mis amigos

9 Me encantaron las vacaciones porque lo pasé ...
  a aburrido
  b bomba
  c autobús

Read the email and complete it with the appropriate verbs from the box.

tenemos	fue	hizo	nos relajamos	me encantaron
voy	fui	comer	pasé	hicimos	fuiste
nos alojamos	comimos	se pueden	nos contaron

¡Hola Quique!
Como sabes, normalmente no (1) _____ de vacaciones al extranjero porque en casa no (2) _____ suficiente dinero pero el año pasado (3) _____ a Colombia con el colegio y (4) _____ en tiendas de campaña en la selva amazónica. ¡(5) _____ muchísimo calor!
En Colombia (6) _____ ver pájaros y plantas muy exóticos y se puede (7) _____ fruta deliciosa como mangos y papayas. Todos los días (8) _____ excursiones por la selva y un día (9) _____ insectos y serpientes. ¡(10) _____ horrible!
Por las noches (11) _____ al lado del fuego y los guías (12) _____ historias fantásticas de estas tierras. ¡(13) _____ las vacaciones y lo (14) _____ fenomenal!
¿Y tú? ¿ (15) _____ de vacaciones el verano pasado?
Un abrazo
Pepe

Respond to Pepe's email.

NC 5–6

Los jóvenes – ¿vemos demasiado la televisión?

 **Tele-chica** Mi mamá me dice todo el tiempo: ¡ves demasiado la televisión! Pero yo veo solamente una o dos horas la noche. En mi opinión no es mucho. ¿Qué pensáis?

 **Marta la rosa** Pues, bien. Pero a mí no me gusta hacer deporte. Ver la televisión es muy divertido. No es un problema.

 **Juan jo 23** ¿Dos horas cada noche? Me parece mucho. ¿Cuándo haces los deberes?

 **Madrileño** Estoy de acuerdo con Juan jo 23. No está bien por la salud ver la televisión todo el día. Por eso hay mucha gente gorda en España.

 **Tele-chica** Juan jo 23, eres muy aburrido. No me interesan los deberes.

 **Marta la rosa** ¡¡No soy gorda!!

 **Marta la rosa** Estoy de acuerdo, Tele-chica. ¡En mi casa vemos la televisión desde las siete de la mañana hasta las once de la noche!

 **Madrileño** Si ves la televisión todo el día, vas a ser gorda.

 **Juan jo 23** Eso es ridículo. Prefiero hacer deporte o ir al café con mis amigos.

 **Marta la rosa** ¡Tú no eres muy simpático!

 Read and decide. Who:

1 watches TV all day?
2 prefers sport?
3 watches TV for one or two hours a day?
4 thinks watching TV is fun?
5 thinks watching too much TV is bad for your health?
6 thinks it's silly to watch TV all day?
7 thinks if you watch too much TV you'll get fat?

en mi opinión	no está bien
estoy de acuerdo	por eso
gordo/a	si
la salud	

 What do you think of what Madrileño said to Marta la rosa? Was he rude or truthful? What would you do if someone said something you didn't like when you were on the internet?

Gramática

Introduction

In order to speak or write correctly in a language, we need to know the grammar basics behind the construction of sentences. The ability to identify patterns and to understand and apply grammar rules in Spanish allows you to use the language to say what you want to say.

In this section you will find a summary of the main grammar points covered by this book with some activities to check that you have understood and can use the language accurately.

Glossary of terms

noun *un sustantivo* = a person, animal, object, place or thing

*Pablo navega por **internet** en el **ordenador** de su **dormitorio**.*

determiner *un determinante* = a little word before a noun to introduce it or modify it

***un** perro, **unos** CDs, **la** casa, **mi** hermano*

singular *el singular* = one of something

***un** gato, **la** cocina*

plural *el plural* = two or more of something

***unos** gatos, **las** serpientes, **tres** elefantes*

pronoun *un pronombre* = a little word used to replace a noun or a name

***Él** juega al fútbol. **Ellas** van al cine.*

verb *un verbo* = a 'doing' or 'being' word

***Hablo** español. **Estudias** francés. **Somos** deportistas. **Van** al cine. **Odio** la lectura.*

tense *el tiempo verbal* = tells you when the action takes place

*Normalmente **voy** en autobús. Ayer **fui** a pie. Mañana **voy a ir** en coche.*

adjective *un adjetivo* = a describing word

*Mi madre es **simpática**. La cocina es **grande**.*

preposition *una preposición* = tells you the position of someone or something

*El cine está **delante** del restaurante. El perro está **en** el jardín.*

Gramática

1 Nouns and determiners

1.1 Nouns

All nouns in Spanish are either masculine or feminine. Most nouns ending in **o** are masculine and most ending in **a** are feminine.

libro → masculine   *biblioteca* → feminine

1.2 Making the plural

Add an **-s** to nouns ending in a vowel and **-es** to words ending in a consonant.

un perro → *dos perros*
un profesor → *dos profesores*

1.3 Determiners (the, a, an, some)

Determiners in Spanish change depending on the gender (masculine/feminine) and number (singular/plural) of the noun they precede.

the (definite article):

	masculine	feminine
singular	el	la
plural	los	las

a/an/some (indefinite article):

	masculine	feminine
singular	un	una
plural	unos	unas

When you learn a new noun, it is a good idea to learn it together with the determiner, particularly if it doesn't end in **-o** or **-a**; so that you know whether it is masculine or feminine.

the tree → **el** *árbol*   **the** trees → **los** *árbol***es**
a tree → **un** *árbol*   **some** trees → **unos** *árbol***es**

the flower → **la** *flor*   **the** flower**s** → **las** *flor***es**
a flower → **una** *flor*   **some** flower**s** → **unas** *flor***es**

A Are these nouns masculine or feminine?

la estación → *feminine*   un árbol

un animal   el camión   el carnaval

una canción   una bandera   el accidente

la visión   un jardín

B Make the plural of the nouns in Activity A. Remember to change the determiners as well as the ending of the nouns.

la estación → *las estaciones*

2 Adjectives

Adjectives are words we use to describe nouns.
In Spanish:

- They generally go after the noun: the white house → *la casa blanca*
- They always match the gender and number of the noun they describe:
  un *perr***o** *negr***o** **but** *un***a** *rat***a** *negr***a**
  un *gat***o** *blanc***o** **but** *un***os** *gat***os** *blanc***os**

To make the feminine of adjectives:

If the masc. ends in:	The feminine form:	
-o	changes to -a	**un** *libro* rojo → **una** *revista* roja
-l, -s, -e, -n (except nationalities)	There is no change	**un** *balón* gris → **una** *pelota* gris *but* **un** *chico* inglés → **una** *chica* inglesa
-r	Add an -a	**un** *niño* hablador → **una** *niña* habladora
-a (some exceptions like *rosa*)	There is no change	**un** *joven* deportista → **una** *joven* deportista

To make the plural of adjectives follow the same rules as for making the plural of nouns: add **-s** to adjectives ending in a vowel and **-es** to adjectives ending in consonants.

black	masculine	feminine
singular	negro	negra
plural	negros	negras

charming	masculine	feminine
singular	encantador	encantadora
plural	encantadores	encantadoras

C How would you say these in Spanish?

1 a small house → *una casa pequeña*
2 a charming girl
3 a small cat
4 a modern kitchen
5 a chatty boy
6 an intelligent student
7 a big garden
8 a red book
9 a yellow car
10 an English teacher

D Make the plural of the phrases in Activity C.

una casa pequeña → *unas casas pequeñas*

3 Possessives

3.1 The possessive of nouns

Beware! In Spanish, structures such as 'my father's car' which have an apostrophe ('s) do not exist.

To show who or what something or someone belongs to use *de* (of) with the noun.

*el coche **de** mi padre* → the car **of** my father → my father's car

 Note that ***de** + **el** = **del*** → *el comedor **del** instituto*

3.2 Possessive adjectives

Possessive adjectives show who or what something belongs to (my school, your books, his family etc.).

They come before the noun they describe and like all adjectives, they have to match the noun they describe.

		singular (one thing *owned*)	plural (two or more things *owned*)
singular (1 owner)	my	mi	mis
	your	tu	tus
	his/her/your (formal)	su	sus
plural (2 or more owners)	our	nuestro (*what is owned is masculine*) nuestra (*what is owned is feminine*)	nuestros (*what is owned is masculine*) nuestras (*what is owned is feminine*)
	your (plural)	vuestro (*what is owned is masculine*) vuestra (*what is owned is feminine*)	vuestros (*what is owned is masculine*) vuestras (*what is owned is feminine*)
	their/your (formal plural)	su	sus

For example:

My father is taller than your mother. → *Mi padre es más alto que tu madre.*

Our mother speaks to your brothers. → *Nuestra **madre** habla con tus hermanos.*

> **E Translate into Spanish.**
>
> 1 your (sing.) dog → *tu perro*
> 2 our family
> 3 their car
> 4 his house
> 5 your (plural) school bags
> 6 my teachers
> 7 our sisters
> 8 her grandmother
> 9 their CDs
> 10 our computers

4 Prepositions

Prepositions are words that specify time, direction or place.

a → at   *Empieza **a** las tres.* → It starts **at** three.

de → from   *Viene **de** la piscina.* → He comes **from** the swimming pool.

en → in   *José está **en** el instituto.* → José is **in** school.

 Note that in Spanish, prepositions are generally followed by the definite article:

*a + el = **al*** → *Voy **a** la piscina* **but** *Voy **al** instituto*

*de + el = **del*** → *Vengo **de** la piscina* **but** *Vengo **del** instituto*

4.1 Simple prepositions

These consist of one word only: ***a*** (at, to), ***de*** (of, from), ***sobre*** (on), ***en*** (in), ***entre*** (between), etc.

*Los deberes están **sobre** la mesa.* → The homework is **on** the table.

4.2 Compound prepositions

These require more than one word in order to be grammatically correct. In Spanish, most prepositions of place are compound prepositions because they require ***de***:

delante de → in front of
detrás de → behind
enfrente de → opposite
debajo de → under
al lado de → next to
a la derecha de → to the right of
a la izquierda de → to the left of

> **F Where are the pets?**
>
> Example: *El pájaro grande está en el armario.*
>
>

5 Subject pronouns

The subject of a sentence tells you who or what is doing the action. We use subject pronouns to replace nouns or names and avoid repetition:

Anna is washing her hair; **she** will call you back in a while.
The exam was difficult. **It** was very long too.

Singular (subject is on his/her/ its own)	I	yo
	you	tú
	he/she/it	él/ella/-
Plural (action is done by two or more subjects)	we	nosotros/nosotras
	you	vosotros/vosotras
	they	ellos/ellas

- In Spanish we don't have 'it' because all nouns are either masculine or feminine.
- Use masculine pronouns to refer to masculine subjects and feminine to refer to feminine subjects. When talking about a mixed group, use the masculine even when masculine is a minority within the group.

6 Verbs

6.1 The infinitive

The infinitive is the original form of a verb and often the only one you will find in the dictionary.

In English the infinitive form is the one that has 'to' in front: to cook, to read, to write, etc. In Spanish infinitives end in -ar, -er, or -ir: cocin**ar**, le**er**, escrib**ir**.

Spanish infinitives are made of a stem + an ending.

stem	ending
estudi	-ar
com	-er
viv	-ir

The infinitive of a verb is extremely important as it is your starting point if you are to use verbs correctly.

G Identify the infinitives. Copy them and highlight the endings. What do they mean?

comedor cantar —to sing ganador trabajador toro puerto volcán subir sal pintar ordenador estudiar dormir dibujo ganar trabajar volver salir estudio

6.2 Present tense of regular verbs

The present tense describes actions which take place regularly or are taking place at this moment in time:

I go to school (every day) / **I am going** to school (right now)

Unlike English, in Spanish you have a different ending for each subject pronoun. This means that subject pronouns can and most often are omitted without the sentence becoming unclear.

	hablar (to speak)	comer (to eat)	vivir (to live)
(yo)	habl**o** (I speak)	com**o** (I eat)	viv**o** (I live)
(tú)	habl**as** (you speak)	com**es** (you eat)	viv**es** (you live)
(él/ella/Ud.*)	habl**a** (he/she/it/you speak[s])	com**e** (he/she/it/you eat[s])	viv**e** (he/she/it/you live[s])
(nosotros/as)	habl**amos** (we speak)	com**emos** (we eat)	viv**imos** (we live)
(vosotros/as)	habl**áis** (you [plural] speak)	com**éis** (you [plural] eat)	viv**ís** (you [plural] live)
(ellos/as/Uds.*)	habl**an** (they/you speak)	com**en** (they/you eat)	viv**en** (they/you live)

* Ud. (Usted) and Uds. (Ustedes) are polite forms used when speaking to someone older that you need or want to show respect to. They take the third ending singular or plural.

Regular verbs follow a clear pattern so you only need to know one verb of each ending (-ar, -er, -ir). In order to work out any regular verb, follow these simple 1, 2, 3 rules:

1 Identify which column you need according to the ending of the infinitive of your new verb (-ar, -er or -ir).

See Zoom OxBox

2   Identify which row you need by working out you who is talking or being talked about (I, you, he/she/it, we, you, they).

3   Remove the ending of your new verb and replace it with the new ending found where your column and row meet.

For 'they work' you need the infinitive 'to work' → *trabajar*.

1   *Trabajar* will follow the same pattern as *hablar* as it is an *-ar* verb.

2   You will need the last row as it is the one referring to 'they' (*ellos*).

3   They work → (*ellos*) *trabaj+an* → *trabajan*

H   How would you say in Spanish ...?

1   we go out (*salir*) → *salimos*
2   he avoids (*evitar*)
3   you (sing.) eat (*comer*)
4   they learn (*aprender*)
5   I sing (*cantar*)
6   we change (*cambiar*)
7   you (plural) describe (*describir*)
8   you (plural) lose (*perder*)
9   you (formal) need (*necesitar*)
10   we return (*volver*)

6.3   Past tense of regular verbs

To describe actions that have already happened and so are in the past, we use a tense known as the preterite:

I **studied** for my exam. I **ate** chips.

In English one form of the verb suits all pronouns:
I talked, you talked, he/she/it talked, we talked, you (plural) talked, they talked. Once again, this doesn't happen in Spanish and each subject pronoun has its own ending.

	hablar (to speak)	comer (to eat)	vivir (to live)
(yo)	habl**é** (I spoke)	com**í** (I ate)	viv**í** (I lived)
(tú)	habl**aste** (you spoke)	com**iste** (you ate)	viv**iste** (you lived)
(él/ella/Ud.)	habl**ó** (he/she/it/you spoke)	com**ió** (he/she/it/you ate)	viv**ió** (he/she/it/you lived)
(nosotros/as)	habl**amos** (we spoke)	com**imos** (we ate)	viv**imos** (we lived)
(vosotros/as)	habl**asteis** (you [plural] spoke)	com**isteis** (you [plural] ate)	viv**isteis** (you [plural] lived)
(ellos/as/Uds.)	habl**aron** (they/you spoke)	com**ieron** (they ate)	viv**ieron** (they/you lived)

You can work out the ending you need by following the same 1, 2, 3 rules as for the present tense but make sure that you are using a preterite tense table!

I   Complete the sentences with the correct form of the preterite.

1   Elías y Jorge *jugaron* al fútbol en el parque. (jugar)
2   Nosotros _____ una película romántica. (ver)
3   Mamá _____ espaguetis para la cena. (cocinar)
4   Juan y yo _____ la idea al profesor. (sugerir)
5   Mi hermana _____ en una oficina el verano pasado. (trabajar)
6   Vosotros _____ tarde a la fiesta. (llegar)

6.4   Reflexive verbs

When you look up a reflexive verb in a dictionary you will find its infinitive has **-se** after the *-ar*, *-er* or *-ir*: *llamarse, ponerse, vestirse*.

The *-se* needs to be removed from the end and brought to the front of the verb as a reflexive pronoun which will take a different form for each subject pronoun: *me, te, se, nos, os, se*.

You then work out the ending of the verb as you would if it was any other verb.

*duch**arse*** → to have a shower

*me duch**o*** → I have a shower

*te duch**as*** → you have a shower

*se duch**a*** → he/she has a shower

*nos duch**amos*** → we have a shower

*os duch**áis*** → you (plural) have a shower

*se duch**an*** → they have a shower

J   Write the correct form of the verb and work out the meaning using a dictionary if necessary.

1   me (levantarse) → *me levanto* → *I get up*
2   nos (peinarse)
3   se (afeitarse)
4   nos (despertarse)
5   os (preocuparse)
6   te (maquillarse)
7   nos (acostarse)
8   me (enojarse)

See Zoom OxBox

Gramática

6.5 Stem-changing verbs (or radical-changing verbs)

A small number of verbs follow the rules of regular verbs but there is also a change in the stem in the present tense.

jugar (to play) → *ju**e**go* (I play)

*pref**e**rir* (to prefer) → *pref**ie**ro* (I prefer)

When a verb is stem-changing, you need to remember the pattern 1, 2, 3, 6 as these persons change:

v**o**lver	despertarse*
(1) v**ue**lvo	(1) me desp**ie**rto
(2) v**ue**lves	(2) te desp**ie**rtas
(3) v**ue**lve	(3) se desp**ie**rta
(4) volvemos	(4) nos despertamos
(5) volvéis	(5) os despertáis
(6) v**ue**lven	(6) se desp**ie**rtan

*Despertarse is stem-changing and reflexive.

6.6 Irregular verbs

Irregular verbs don't follow any given pattern and so they need to be learnt in full. Here are some examples:

present tense				
ser to be (permanent)	**estar** to be (temporary or location)	**hacer** (to do/to make)	**tener** (to have)	**ir** (to go)
soy	estoy	hago	tengo	voy
eres	estás	haces	tienes	vas
es	está	hace	tiene	va
somos	estamos	hacemos	tenemos	vamos
sois	estáis	hacéis	tenéis	vais
son	están	hacen	tienen	van

preterite (past) tense				
ser	**estar**	**hacer**	**tener**	**ir**
fui	estuve	hice	tuve	fui
fuiste	estuviste	hiciste	tuviste	fuiste
fue	estuvo	hizo	tuvo	fue
fuimos	estuvimos	hicimos	tuvimos	fuimos
fuisteis	estuvisteis	hicisteis	tuvisteis	fuisteis
fueron	estuvieron	hicieron	tuvieron	fueron

K **How would you say these in Spanish?**

1 I went to the cinema. →
  Fui al cine.
2 They have an exam.
3 She is intelligent.
4 The car is in the garage.
5 We did the homework.
6 You go to school.

6.7 Immediate future

The immediate future means '**going to do** something', e.g. '**I am going to go** to the cinema'.

To form the immediate future use the following formula:

present tense of verb to go (*ir*) + *a* + infinitive form of the verb

Examples:

Voy a hablar/comer/salir …	I am going to speak/eat/go out …
Vas a hablar/comer/salir …	you are going to speak/eat/go out …
Va a hablar/comer/salir …	he/she is going to speak/eat/go out …
Vamos a hablar/comer/salir …	we are going to speak/eat/go out …
Vais a hablar/comer/salir …	you (plural) are going to speak/eat/go out …
Van a hablar/comer/salir …	they are going to speak/eat/go out …

L **Rewrite these sentences in the immediate future.**

1 Voy al instituto todos los días. →
  Voy a ir al instituto todos los días.
2 Jugamos al fútbol durante el recreo.
3 Escucho música en mi dormitorio.
4 Van al cine con sus padres.
5 Veo mi programa favorito a las seis.
6 Aprende español en el instituto.

6.8 Imperative

The imperative is used when you are telling somebody to do something or giving them an order.

The Spanish imperative exists for five different grammatical people: *tú, usted, nosotros, vosotros* and *ustedes*. The *nosotros* form is less commonly used than the others.

⚠️ Positive and negative commands have different endings for the informal forms.

To form the imperative:
Take the *-ar*, *-er* or *-ir* ending and replace it with the relevant ending from the table:

See Zoom OxBox

	-ar e.g. *hablar*		-er e.g. *comer*		-ir e.g. *escribir*	
	positive	negative	positive	negative	positive	negative
tú	¡Habl**a**!	¡No habl**es**!	¡Com**e**!	¡No com**as**!	¡Escrib**e**!	¡No escrib**as**!
usted	¡Habl**e**!	¡No habl**e**!	¡Com**a**!	¡No com**a**!	¡Escrib**a**!	¡No escrib**a**!
vosotros/as	¡Habl**ad**!	¡No habl**éis**!	¡Com**ed**!	¡No com**áis**!	¡Escrib**id**!	¡No escrib**áis**!
ustedes	¡Habl**en**!	¡No habl**en**!	¡Com**an**!	¡No com**an**!	¡Escrib**an**!	¡No escrib**an**!

M Write the correct form of the imperative to complete these sentences.

Example: **1** Hablad

1 ¡ _____ con el profesor! (hablar, vosotros)
2 ¡ _____ a tu madre! (preguntar, tú)
3 ¡No _____ las escaleras! (subir, Uds)
4 ¡No _____ en clase! (beber, vosotros)
5 ¡No _____ en el examen! (copiar, tú)
6 ¡Por favor _____ a su secretaria! (llamar, Ud)

7 Negatives

To make a sentence negative, place the word **no** before the verb:

Tengo hermanos → No tengo hermanos.

When the answer to a question is negative, the word *no* appears twice:

¿Tienes animales? No, no tengo animales.

N Write sentences saying the opposite.

1 Tiene una hermana. → *No tiene una hermana.*
2 Me gustan los idiomas.
3 Tengo un bolígrafo.
4 En la ciudad hay discotecas.
5 Me gusta el chocolate.
6 En verano, voy de vacaciones con mis padres.

8 Asking questions

In Spanish there is no difference in the word order of statements and questions. For this reason it is important that:
- When writing, in addition to the question mark at the end, you must also write an upside down question mark at the beginning of your question: ¿ ... ?
- When speaking, you make your voice go up at the end of the sentence:

Statement:
You like animals.
Te gustan los animales.

Question:
Do you like animals?
¿Te gustan los animales?

All Spanish question words have accents:
¿Quién/Quiénes ...? Who ...?
¿Qué ...? What ...?
¿Cuál/Cuáles ...? Which ...?
¿Dónde ...? Where ...?
¿Adónde ...? Where (to) ...?
¿Cuándo ...? When ...?
¿Cuánto/cuánta/cuántos/cuántas ...? How much/How many ...?
¿Cómo ...? How/What is it like?
¿Por qué ...? Why ...?

O What is the question for each of these answers?

1 Me llamo Sofía. → *¿Cómo te llamas?*
2 Quiero patatas fritas.
3 Porque tengo un examen mañana.
4 Sí, me gusta el español.
5 Mi casa tiene tres dormitorios.
6 Mi instituto es muy antiguo.

9 Opinions

Opinions such as *me gusta* or *me interesa* don't end in an **o** for the present tense when talking about 'myself' because they actually translate as 'it pleases me' and 'it interests me'. Effectively the ending matches 'it' (third person singular). This is why when what you like is plural, e.g. *las matemáticas*, we say *me gust**an*** ('they please me').

When you talk about other people's likes and dislikes the pronoun changes: *me, te, le, nos, os, les.*

Example: *te gusta(n)* → you like (it/they please(s) you), *nos gusta(n)* → we like (it/they please(s) us).

When the opinion is followed by a noun, the definite article is needed:
- *Me gustan **las** ciencias. No me gusta **el** fútbol.*

When the opinion is folllowed by a verb, you must use its infinitive form:
- *Me gusta cocin**ar**. Me gusta aprend**er** idiomas.*

Gramática

10 Comparative and superlative

In order to make comparisons in Spanish you will need to use:

- *más/menos* + adjective + *que* ... → more/less … than …
  *El zumo es **más sano que** la Coca-Cola.* Juice is healthier than Coke.

- *tan* + adjective + *como* ... → as ... as ...
  *El examen de ciencias fue **tan difícil como** el de historia.* The science exam was as difficult as the history one.

- *el/la/los/las más/menos* + adjective → the most/least ...
  *Alicia es **la menos deportista** del grupo.* Alicia is the least sporty of the group.

 Remember that there are some common irregular comparatives and superlatives:

bueno → *mejor que, el/la mejor*

malo → *peor que, el/la peor*

viejo (referring to people) → *mayor que, el/la mayor*

joven → *menor que, el/la menor*

> **P** **How would you say these in Spanish?**
>
> 1 Bea is more elegant than Sofía. → *Bea es más elegante que Sofía.*
> 2 Jorge is younger than Pedro.
> 3 Silvia is less shy than Carmen.
> 4 Rubén is the least responsible.
> 5 Jana is the most beautiful.
> 6 Playing tennis is more fun than swimming.

11 Adverbs

Adverbs are words that describe or modify verbs.

Most Spanish adverbs are formed by adding *-mente* to the feminine singular form of the adjective.

adjective			adverb	
	masculine	feminine		
fast	rápido	rápida	rápidamente	quickly
generous	generoso	generosa	generosamente	generously
clear	claro	clara	claramente	clearly
difficult	difícil	difícil	difícilmente	with difficulty
normal	normal	normal	normalmente	normally
affectionate	cariñoso	cariñosa	cariñosamente	affectionately

 Bastante (quite), *demasiado* (too), *mucho* (a lot), *muy* (very), *nunca* (never), *poco* (little) and *siempre* (always) are common adverbs that don't follow the pattern.

Expresiones útiles

Learn the days of the week, months and seasons, plus all the numbers to 100 by heart.

Numbers 100–3000		Los números 100–3000	
100	cien, ciento	700	setecientos
101	ciento uno	800	ochocientos
110	ciento diez	900	novecientos
200	doscientos	1000	mil
300	trescientos	1001	mil uno
400	cuatrocientos	1215	mil doscientos quince
500	quinientos	2000	dos mil
600	seiscientos	3000	tres mil

Quantifiers	Adverbios de cantidad
a little	un poco
quite	bastante
a lot	mucho/mucha/muchos/muchas
very	muy
too	demasiado

Frequency words	Expresiones de frecuencia
sometimes	a veces
from time to time	de vez en cuando
always	siempre
never	nunca
every day	todos los días
often	a menudo
rarely	raramente

Connectives	Conectores
because	porque/pues/ya que
but	pero
although	aunque
however	sin embargo
in addition	además

Sequencing	Adverbios de secuencia
before	antes (de)
later	más tarde/luego
afterwards/after	después/después de
then	entonces

 See Zoom OxBox

Answers to grammar activities

A

la estación → fem   un árbol → masc   un animal → masc
el camión → masc

el carnaval → masc   una canción → fem
una bandera → fem   el accidente → masc

la visión → fem   un jardín → masc

B

las estaciones, unos árboles, unos animales, unos camiones,
los carnavales, unas canciones, unas banderas, los accidentes,
las visiones, unos jardines

C

1 una casa pequeña **2** una chica encantadora **3** un gato
pequeño **4** una cocina moderna **5** un chico hablador **6** un
estudiante inteligente **7** un jardín grande **8** un libro rojo **9** un
coche amarillo **10** un profesor inglés

D

1 unas casas pequeñas **2** unas chicas encantadoras **3** unos
gatos pequeños **4** unas cocinas modernas **5** unos chicos
habladores **6** unos estudiantes inteligentes **7** unos jardines
grandes **8** unos libros rojos **9** unos coches amarillos **10** unos
profesores ingleses

E

1 tu perro **2** nuestra familia **3** su coche **4** su casa **5** vuestras
mochilas **6** mis profesores **7** nuestras hermanas **8** su abuela
9 sus CDs **10** nuestros ordenadores

F

La serpiente está dentro de la cómoda.
El ratón está en las estanterías.
El pájaro grande está en el armario.
El caballo está detrás de la ventana.
El pez y el conejo están encima del televisor.
El pájaro pequeno está delante del televisor.
El perro está debajo del escritorio.
El gato está en la cama.

G

cantar – to sing, subir – to go up, pintar – to paint, estudiar –
to study, trabajar – to work, dormir – to sleep, ganar – to win
or to earn, salir – to go out, volver – to return

H

1 salimos **2** evita **3** comes **4** aprenden **5** canto **6** cambiamos
7 describís **8** perdéis **9** necesita **10** volvemos

I

1 jugaron **2** vimos **3** cocinó **4** sugerimos **5** trabajó
6 llegasteis

J

1 me levanto → I get up **2** nos peinamos → we brush our
hair **3** se afeita/se afeitan → he shaves/they shave
4 nos despertamos → we wake up **5** os preocupáis → you
(plural) worry **6** te maquillas → you put make-up on **7** nos
acostamos → we go to bed **8** me enojo → I get annoyed

K

1 Fui al cine. **2** Tienen un examen. **3** Ella es inteligente.
4 El coche está en el garaje. **5** Hicimos los deberes.
6 Vas al instituto.

L

1 Voy a ir al instituto todos los días. **2** Vamos a jugar al fútbol
durante el recreo. **3** Voy a escuchar música en mi dormitorio.
4 Van a ir al cine con sus padres. **5** Voy a ver mi programa
favorito a las seis. **6** Va a aprender español en el instituto.

M

1 Hablad **2** Pregunta **3** suban **4** bebáis **5** copies **6** llame

N

1 No tiene una hermana. **2** No me gustan los idiomas.
3 No tengo bolígrafo. **4** En la ciudad no hay discotecas.
5 No me gusta el chocolate. **6** En verano, no voy de
vacaciones con mis padres.

O

1 ¿Cómo te llamas? **2** ¿Qué quieres? **3** ¿Por qué estudias?
4 ¿Te gusta el español? **5** ¿Cuántos dormitorios tiene tu casa?
6 ¿Cómo es tu instituto?

P

2 Jorge es menor que Pedro. **3** Silvia es menos tímida que
Carmen. **4** Rubén es el menos responsable. **5** Jana es la
más bonita. **6** Jugar al tenis es más divertido que practicar
la natación.

Glosario

A

el **abanico** *nm* fan
el **abrazo** *nm* hug
abril April
abrir *vb* to open
la **abuela** *nf* grandmother
el **abuelo** *nm* grandfather
los **abuelos** *nmpl* grandparents
me **aburre** it bores me (from **aburrir**)
aburrido/a *adj* boring
el **aceite** *nm* oil
la **aceituna** *nf* olive
acogedor(a) *adj* cosy
acostarse *vb* to go to bed
la **actividad** *nf* activity
de **acuerdo** in agreement
además *adv* in addition
adiós goodbye
las **afueras** *nfpl* outskirts
agosto August
le **agradezco** thank you (formal, from **agradecer**)
el **agua mineral** *nf* mineral water
al **aire libre** outdoors
el **ajedrez** *nm* chess
el **ajo** *nm* garlic
el **albergue juvenil** *nm* youth hostel
las **albóndigas** *nfpl* meatballs
el **alcázar** *nm* fortress
la **aldea** *nf* village
alejarse *vb* to move away
el **alemán** *nm* German
alemán/alemana *adj* German
Alemania *nf* Germany
la **alfombra** *nf* rug
algo something; **¿algo más?** anything else?
allá *adv* (over) there
allí *adv* there

la **almohada** *nf* pillow
almorzar *vb* to have lunch
almuerzo I have lunch (from **almorzar**)
el **alojamiento** *nm* accommodation
alojarse *vb* to lodge, to stay
alquilar *vb* to hire
alto/a *adj* tall
amarillo/a *adj* yellow
americano/a *adj* American
la **amiga** *nf* friend (female)
el **amigo** *nm* friend (male)
la **amistad** *nf* friendship
el **amor** *nm* love
animado/a *adj* lively
antes de before
de **anticipo** in advance
antiguo/a *adj* old
antipático/a *adj* unfriendly
el **anuncio** *nm* advertisement
el **año** *nm* year
me **apasiona** I adore
aprender *vb* to learn
aquí *adv* here
la **araña** *nf* spider
el **armario** *nm* wardrobe
el **arroz** *nm* rice
el **ascensor** *nm* lift
el **aseo** *nm* toilet
el **asesinato** *nm* murder
la **asignatura** *nf* school subject
el **atentado** *nm* attack
el **ático** *nm* attic
el **atletismo** *nm* athletics
atraer *vb* to attract
el **atún** *nm* tuna
el **aula** *nf* classroom
aunque although
el **autobús** *nm* bus
el **avión** *nm* plane

ayer *adv* yesterday
el **ayuntamiento** *nm* town hall
el **azúcar** *nm* sugar
azul *adj* blue

B

bailar *vb* to dance
bajo/a *adj* short
el **balcón** *nm* balcony
el **baloncesto** *nm* basketball
el **banco** *nm* bank, bench
bañarse *vb* to bathe; to have a bath
barato/a *adj* cheap
la **barba** *nf* beard
el **barrio** *nm* district
bastante *adv* quite
batallar *vb* to fight
beber *vb* to drink
la **bebida** *nf* drink
el **béisbol** *nm* baseball
la **belleza** *nf* beauty
la **biblioteca** *nf* library
la **bicicleta** *nf* bicycle
bien *adv* well
el **bigote** *nm* moustache
el **billete** *nm* ticket
blanco/a *adj* white
el **bloque de pisos** *nm* block of flats
bobo/a *adj* silly
el **bocadillo** *nm* sandwich
la **bolera** *nf* bowling alley
los **bombones** *nmpl* sweets
bonito/a *adj* pretty, nice
la **botella** *nf* bottle
el **boxeo** *nm* boxing
el **buceo** *nm* diving
bueno/a *adj* good
el **burro** *nm* donkey
buscar *vb* to look for

C

el **caballo** *nm* horse
la **cabra** *nf* goat

el **café** *nm* coffee
la **caja** *nf* box
los **calamares** *nmpl* squid
los **calcetines** *nmpl* socks
la **calle** *nf* street
el **calor** *nm* heat
la **cama** *nf* bed
el **camaleón** *nm* chameleon
la **campaña** *nf* countryside
la **camisa** *nf* shirt
la **camiseta** *nf* T-shirt
la **cancha** *nf* **de tenis** tennis court
el **canguro** *nm* kangaroo
la **cantante** *nf* singer
cariñoso/a *adj* affectionate
la **carne** *nf* meat
caro/a *adj* expensive
la **carta** *nf* letter
la **casa** *nf* house
casado/a *adj* married
casarse *vb* to get married
casi *adv* almost
castaño/a *adj* chestnut
las **castañuelas** *nfpl* castanets
el **castillo** *nm* castle
el **catalán** *nm* Catalan
la **catedral** *nf* cathedral
catorce fourteen
la **cebolla** *nf* onion
cenar *vb* to have supper/dinner
el **centro comercial** *nm* shopping centre
cepillarse *vb* to brush (your hair)
cerca *adv* (**de**) near (to)
el **cerdo** *nm* pig
los **cereales** *nmpl* cereal
la **cerveza** *nf* beer
el **chalet** *nm* bungalow

See Zoom OxBox

el **chándal** *nm* tracksuit

charlar *vb* to chat

los **chats** *nmpl* chat rooms

la **chica** *nf* girl

el **chico** *nm* boy

me **chifla** I'm crazy about

el **chorizo** *nm* spicy sausage

los **churros** *nmpl* fritters

el **ciclismo** *nm* cycling

cien a hundred

las **ciencias** *nfpl* science

cinco five

cincuenta fifty

el **cine** *nm* cinema

la **ciudad** *nf* city

claro *adv* clearly

el/la **cliente** *nm/f* customer

la **cobaya** *nf* guinea pig

el **coche** *nm* car

la **cocina** *nf* kitchen

cocinar *vb* to cook

el **cocodrilo** *nm* crocodile

el **colegio** *nm* school

colombiano/a *adj* Colombian

la **comedia** *nf* comedy

el **comedor** *nm* canteen

comenzar *vb* to begin

comer *vb* to eat

la **comida** *nf* lunch; food

la **comida** *nf* **rápida** fast food

¿cómo? how?

la **cómoda** *nf* chest of drawers

cómodo/a *adj* comfortable

complicado/a *adj* complicated

la **compra** *nf* shopping

comprar *vb* to buy

comprender *vb* to understand

con with

el **concurso** *nm* game show

el **conejo** *nm* rabbit

conocer *vb* to know

consigo with him/her

contiene it contains (from **contener**)

la **corbata** *nf* tie

correcto/a *adj* right

el **correo electrónico** *nm* email

la **corrida** *nf* bullfight

las **cortinas** *nfpl* curtains

corto/a *adj* short

la **costa** *nf* coast

creer *vb* to believe

cruza cross (from **cruzar**)

(de) cuadros *adj* checked

¿cuándo? when?

cuarenta forty

el **cuarto de baño** *nm* bathroom

cuatro four

la **cuchara** *nf* spoon

el **cuchillo** *nm* knife

cuesta it costs (from **costar**)

el **cumpleaños** *nm* birthday

D

me **da igual** I don't mind

danés/danesa *adj* Danish

dar *vb* to give

debajo de *prep* under

deber *vb* to have to

los **deberes** *nmpl* homework

decir *vb* to say

el **delfín** *nm* dolphin

delgado/a *adj* slim

delicioso/a *adj* delicious

demasiado *adv* too (much)

dentro de *prep* inside

el/la **dependiente** *nm/f* shop assistant

el **deporte** *nm* sport

el/la **deportista** *nm/f* sportsman/woman

deportivo/a *adj* sports

la **derecha** *nf* right

el **desastre** *nm* disaster

desayunar *vb* to have lunch

el **desayuno** *nm* breakfast

descansar *vb* to rest

descubrir *vb* to discover

desde ... hasta from ... to

desordenado/a *adj* untidy

el **despacho** *nm* study

despertarse *vb* to wake up

después afterwards

la **desventaja** *nf* disadvantage

detrás de *prep* behind

el **día** *nm* day; **todos los días** every day

el **diario** *nm* diary

los **dibujos animados** *nmpl* cartoons

el **diccionario** *nm* dictionary

diciembre December

diecinueve nineteen

dieciocho eighteen

dieciséis sixteen

diecisiete seventeen

los **dientes** *nmpl* teeth

diez ten

difícil *adj* difficult

yo **digo** I say/tell (from **decir**)

Dinamarca *nf* Denmark

el **dinero** *nm* money

la **discoteca** *nf* discotheque

divertido/a *adj* amusing, entertaining

divorciado/a *adj* divorced

doce twelve

el **documental** *nm* documentary

domingo Sunday

¿dónde? *adv* where?

donde quieras wherever you like

dormirse *vb* to fall asleep

el **dormitorio** *nm* bedroom

dos two

la **ducha** *nf* shower

ducharse *vb* to have a shower

E

el **edificio** *nm* building

la **educación** *nf* education

educativo/a *adj* educational

por **ejemplo** for example

el **elefante** *nm* elephant

sin **embargo** however

emocionante *adj* exciting

en in; at

enamorarse de *vb* to fall in love with

me **encanta** I love (from **encantar**)

encima de *prep* on top of

encontrar *vb* to find

enero January

enorme *adj* enormous

la **ensalada (verde)** *nf* (green) salad

entonces *adv* then

la **entrada** *nf* entrance hall

entre *prep* between

el **equipo** *nm* team

las **escaleras** *nfpl* stairs

escocés/escocesa *adj* Scottish

Escocia *nf* Scotland

Glosario

escribir *vb* to write
por escrito in writing
el escritorio *nm* desk
escuchar *vb* to listen (to)
el esfuerzo *nm* effort
a eso de around
espacioso/a *adj* spacious
el español *nm* Spanish
español/española *adj* Spanish
las especias *nfpl* spices
el/la espía *nm/f* spy
la esposa *nf* wife
el esposo *nm* husband
el esquí *nm* skiing
la estación *nf* season
Estados Unidos *nmpl* United States
la estancia *nf* stay
las estanterías *nfpl* bookcase, shelves
estar *vb* to be
yo estoy I am (from **estar**)
el este *nm* east
la estrella *nf* star
estricto/a *adj* strict
el/la estudiante *nm/f* student
estudiar *vb* to study
estudioso/a *adj* studious
estúpido/a *adj* stupid
el extranjero *nm* abroad
explicar *vb* to explain
extrovertido/a *adj* outgoing

F

fácil *adj* easy
las facilidades *nfpl* facilities
fácilmente *adv* easily
la falda *nf* skirt
la familia *nf* family

la fantasía *nf* fantasy
me fascina (...) fascinates me
me fastidia (...) bothers me
febrero February
feo/a *adj* ugly
la fiesta *nf* festival; party
el flamenco *nm* flamenco
flexible *adj* easy-going
me flipa I love (...)
de flores *adj* flowery
el folleto *nm* brochure
la foto *nf* photo
el francés *nm* French
Francia *nf* France
frecuentemente *adv* frequently
el frente *nm* front
el frío *nm* cold
frío/a *adj* cold
el fuego *nm* fire
fuera *adv* outside
soy fuerte (en) I'm good (at)
el fútbol *nm* football
el/la futbolista *nm/f* footballer

G

las gafas *nfpl* **de sol** sunglasses
Gales *nm* Wales
galés/galesa *adj* Welsh
la gamba *nf* prawn
el garaje *nm* garage
con gas fizzy; **sin ...** still
el gato *nm* cat
generalmente *adv* generally
la geografía *nf* geography
el gimnasio *nm* gymnasium
gordo/a *adj* fat
el gorila *nm* gorilla
gracias thanks
gracioso/a *adj* amusing

grande *adj* big
los grandes almacenes *nmpl* department store(s)
grandísimo/a *adj* huge
la granja *nf* farm
la grasa *nf* fat
gratis free (of charge)
el griego *nm* Greek
el guaraní *adj* Guarani
guatemalteco/a *adj* Guatemalan
guay *adj* cool
la guerra *nf* war
el/la guía *nm/f* guide
la guitarra *nf* guitar
me gusta(n) I like ...
no me gusta(n) nada ... I don't like ... at all

H

la habitación *nf* room
hablador(a) *adj* talkative
hablar *vb* to speak
hace (dos años) (two years) ago
hacer *vb* to do, to make
yo hago I do; I make (from **hacer**)
tengo hambre I'm hungry
la hamburguesa *nf* hamburger
hasta luego see you later
hasta pronto see you soon
hay there is, there are
el helado *nm* ice cream
la hermana *nf* sister
la hermanastra *nf* half-sister/ stepsister
el hermanastro *nm* half-brother/ stepbrother
el hermano *nm* brother
la hija única *nf* only child (female)

el hijo único *nm* only child (male)
el hipopótamo *nm* hippopotamus
la historia *nf* history; story
la hora *nf* hour
hoy *adv* today

I

de ida y vuelta return (ticket)
el idioma *nm* language
la iglesia *nf* church
la imagen *nf* image
el imán *nm* magnet
impaciente *adj* impatient
impresionante *adj* impressive
incluso *adv* even
incómodo/a *adj* uncomfortable
increíble *adj* incredible
la informática *nf* IT
informativo/a *adj* informative
Inglaterra *nf* England
el inglés *nm* English
inglés/inglesa *adj* English
inmaduro/a *adj* immature
inolvidable *adj* unforgettable
insociable *adj* unsociable
el instituto *nm* secondary school
inteligente *adj* intelligent
el intercambio *nm* exchange
me interesa(n) I'm interested in ...
interesante *adj* interesting
el invierno *nm* winter
ir *vb* to go
Irlanda *nf* Ireland
irlandés/irlandesa *adj* Irish
la isla *nf* island

See Zoom OxBox

el **italiano** *nm* Italian
la **izquierda** *nf* left

J

el **jardín** *nm* garden
el **jersey** *nm* sweater
la **jirafa** *nf* giraffe
jueves Thursday
jugar *vb* to play (game)
el **juguete** *nm* toy
julio July
junio June

L

el **laboratorio** *nm* laboratory
al **lado de** beside, next to
el **ladrón** *nm* thief
lamentablemente *adv* unfortunately
la **lámpara** *nf* lamp
el **lápiz** *nm* pencil
el **largo** *nm* length
largo/a *adj* long
lavarse *vb* to wash (yourself)
la **leche** *nf* milk
leer *vb* to read
lejos de far from
la **lengua** *nf* language
lentamente *adv* slowly
la **letra** *nf* letter
levantarse *vb* to get up
el **libro** *nm* book
limpio/a *adj* clean
liso/a *adj* straight
la **llama** *nf* llama
llamarse *vb* to be called
el **llavero** *nm* key ring
llegar *vb* to arrive
llevar *vb* to wear
llueve it's raining (from **llover**)
loco/a *adj* mad
la **lucha** *nf* struggle
luego then
el **lugar** *nm* place
lunes Monday

M

la **madrastra** *nf* stepmother
la **madre** *nf* mother
maduro/a *adj* mature
voy **mal (en)** I'm bad (at)
mal *adv* badly
malsano/a *adj* unhealthy
sin **mangas** *adj* sleeveless
con **mangas cortas (largas)** *adj* short (long)-sleeved
la **mano** *nf* hand
la **manzana** *nf* apple
mañana *adv* tomorrow
la **mañana** *nf* morning
el **mapa** *nm* map
maravilloso/a *adj* wonderful
el **marido** *nm* husband
los **mariscos** *nmpl* seafood
marrón *adj* brown
marroquí *adj* Moroccan
Marruecos *nm* Morocco
martes Tuesday
marzo March
más more
la **mascota** *nf* pet
las **matemáticas** *nfpl* maths
mayo May
mayor older (age)
la **mayoría** *nf* the majority
la **medianoche** *nf* midnight
el **mediodía** *nm* midday
mejor *adv* better; **el/la/lo mejor** the best
el **melocotón** *nm* peach
menor younger (age)
la **mentira** *nf* lie

a **menudo** *adv* often
el **mercado** *nm* market
merendar *vb* to have tea/an afternoon snack
la **merienda** *nf* (afternoon) snack
la **mermelada** *nf* marmalade; jam
el **mes** *nm* month
la **mesita** *nf* side table
miércoles Wednesday
el **minuto** *nm* minute
mirar *vb* to look at, watch
la **misión** *nf* mission
el/la **mío** mine
la **moda** *nf* fashion
moderno/a *adj* modern
me **mola** I'm into it
me **molesta** it annoys me
las **montañas** *nfpl* mountains
montar *vb* **a caballo** to go horse riding
morado/a *adj* purple
morisco/a *adj* Moorish
la **mosca** *nf* fly
el **móvil** *nm* mobile (phone)
mucho/a *adj* a lot
la **mujer** *nf* woman, wife
el **mundo** *nm* the world
la **muñeca** *nf* doll
el **museo** *nm* museum
la **música** *nf* music
muy *adv* very

N

nacer *vb* to be born
la **nacionalidad** *nf* nationality
nada más only
nada nothing
nadar *vb* to swim
naranja *adj* orange
la **naranja** *nf* orange

navegar *vb* **por internet** to surf the internet
la **Navidad** Christmas
necesitar *vb* to need
negro/a *adj* black
nervioso/a *adj* nervous
nevar *vb* to snow
ni ... ni ... neither ... nor ...
la **niebla** *nf* fog
nieva it's snowing (from **nevar**)
¡ni hablar! out of the question!
los **niños** *nmpl* children
la **noche** *nf* night
el **nombre** *nm* name
el **noreste** *nm* northeast
normalmente *adv* normally
el **noroeste** *nm* northwest
el **norte** *nm* north
las **notas** *nfpl* marks
las **noticias** *nfpl* news
noventa ninety
noviembre November
la **nube** *nf* cloud
nublado/a *adj* cloudy
nuestro/a *adj* our
nueve nine
nunca *adv* never

O

ochenta eighty
ocho eight
octubre October
odiar *vb* to hate
el **oeste** *nm* west
la **oficina** *nf* **(de Correos)** (post) office
ofrecer *vb* to offer
los **ojos** *nmpl* eyes
olvidar *vb* to forget
once eleven
ondulado/a *adj* wavy

Glosario

ordenado/a *adj* tidy

el **osito** *nm* teddy bear

el **otoño** *nm* autumn

otro/a *adj* another

la **oveja** *nf* sheep

P

paciente *adj* patient

el **padrastro** *nm* stepfather

el **padre** *nm* father

los **padres** *nmpl* parents

el **país** *nm* country

el **pájaro** *nm* bird

la **palabra** *nf* word

el **pan** *nm* bread

los **pantalones** *nmpl* trousers

Paquistán *nm* Pakistan

paquistaní *adj* Pakistani

la **parada** *nf* **de autobús** bus stop

el **parador** *nm* tourist hotel

paraguayo/a *adj* Paraguayan

las **paredes** *nfpl* walls

los **parientes** *nmpl* relatives

el **parque (de atracciones)** *nm* (theme) park

participar *vb* to participate

el **partido** *nm* game, match

pasado/a *adj* last

lo **pasamos bomba** we have/had a great time

el **pasatiempo** *nm* pastime

lo **pasé fenomenal/ bomba** I had a great time

pasear *vb* **al perro** to walk the dog

el **pastel** *nm* cake

las **patatas fritas** *nfpl* chips

el **patio** *nm* (school) playground

el **pato** *nm* duck

las **pecas** *nfpl* freckles

pedí I asked for (from **pedir**)

pedir *vb* to ask for

peinarse *vb* to comb (your hair)

la **película** *nf* film

... de acción action film

... de ciencia-ficción sci-fi film

... de guerra war film

... de misterio mystery film

... de terror horror film

... de vaqueros western

peligroso/a *adj* dangerous

pelirrojo/a *adj* red-haired

el **pelo** *nm* hair

la **pelota vasca** *nf* pelota (Basque ball game)

la **pensión** *nf* B&B

peor *adv* worse; **el/ la/lo peor** the worst

pequeño/a *adj* small

perder *vb* to lose

la **pérdida** *nf* **(de tiempo)** waste (of time)

perezoso/a *adj* lazy

el **periódico** *nm* newspaper

pero but

el **perrito caliente** *nm* hot dog

el **perro** *nm* dog

el **pescado** *nm* fish

pescar *vb* to fish

el **pez** *nm* fish

picante *adj* spicy

a **pie** on foot

pintoresco/a *adj* picturesque

la **piña** *nf* pineapple

la **piscina** *nf* swimming pool

el **piso** *nm* apartment; floor

la **planta baja** *nf* ground floor

el **plátano** *nm* banana

la **playa** *nf* beach

poco/a *adj* little

poder *vb* to be able

polaco/a *adj* Polish

policiaco/a *adj* crime (film, novel)

el **polideportivo** *nm* sports centre

el **pollo** *nm* **(asado)** (roast) chicken

Polonia *nf* Poland

ponerse *vb* to put on (clothes)

porque *conj* because

portugués/ portuguesa *adj* Portuguese

la **postal** *nf* postcard

el **póster** *nm* poster

el **postre** *nm* dessert

practicar *vb* to practise; to play (sport)

práctico/a *adj* practical

precioso/a *adj* lovely

preferido/a *adj* favourite

preferir *vb* to prefer

la **prima** *nf* cousin (female)

la **primavera** *nf* spring (season)

la **primera planta** *nf* first floor

primero/a *adj* first

el **primo** *nm* cousin (male)

probablemente *adv* probably

el/la **profe** *nm/f* teacher

el/la **profesor(a)** *nm/f* teacher

el **programa** *nm* programme

el **pueblo** *nm* town

se **puede** you can (from **poder**)

el **puente** *nm* bridge

la **puerta** *nf* door

el **pulpo** *nm* octopus

de **punta** spiky (hair)

en **punto** precisely

de **puntos** *adj* spotted

Q

quedarse *vb* to stay

me lo **quedo** I'll take it

querer *vb* to want

el **queso** *nm* cheese

¿qué tal? how are you?

¡qué va! absolutely not!

¿quién? who?

yo **quiero** I want (from **querer**)

quince fifteen

quizás *adv* perhaps

R

rápidamente *adv* quickly

la **rata** *nf* rat

el **ratón** *nm* mouse

de **rayas** *adj* striped

la **recepción** *nf* reception (desk)

todo **recto** straight on

el **recuerdo** *nm* souvenir

el **regalo** *nm* gift

regular *adj* average

relajarse *vb* to relax

reservar *vb* to reserve

la **revista** *nf* magazine

el **río** *nm* river

rizado/a *adj* curly

robar *vb* to rob

el **robo** *nm* robbery

rojo/a *adj* red

el **ron** *nm* rum

rosa *adj* pink

rubio/a *adj* blond

ruidoso/a *adj* noisy

la **rutina diaria** *nf* daily routine

S

sábado Saturday

la **sábana** *nf* sheet

sacar *vb* to get

la **sal** *nf* salt

See Zoom OxBox

salir *vb* to go out
el **salón** *nm* lounge, living room
¡saludos! greetings!
sano/a *adj* healthy
secreto/a *adj* secret
el **secuestro** *nm* kidnapping
tengo **sed** I'm thirsty
en **seguida** at once
segundo/a *adj* second
seis six
la **semana** *nf* week
sencillo/a *adj* plain
septiembre September
ser *vb* to be
la **serie** *nf* series
la **serpiente** *nf* snake
sesenta sixty
setenta seventy
siempre *adv* always
lo **siento** I'm sorry
siete seven
el **siglo** *nm* century
sigue continue (from **seguir**)
la **silla** *nf* chair
simpático/a *adj* friendly
sin without
se **sirve** is served (from **servir**)
el **sitio** *nm* place
el **sol** *nm* sun
solamente *adv* only
solucionar *vb* to solve
el **sombrero** *nm* hat
no **soporto** I can't stand
soso/a *adj* tasteless
el **sótano** *nm* basement
yo **soy** I am (from **ser**)
su/sus *adj* his/her/your
subir *vb* to go up
sucio/a *adj* dirty
la **sudadera** *nf* sweatshirt
la **suerte** *nf* (good) luck
suficiente *adj* enough

el **supermercado** *nm* supermarket
por **supuesto** of course
el **sur** *nm* south
el **sureste** *nm* southeast
el **suroeste** *nm* southwest

T

de **talla mediana** *adj* of average size
también *adv* also
tan *adv* so
la **tarántula** *nf* tarantula
más **tarde** later
la **tarde** *nf* afternoon, evening
la **televisión** *nf* television
el **tatuaje** *nm* tattoo
la **tecnología** *nf* technology
el **teléfono** *nm* telephone
la **telenovela** *nf* (TV) soap
el **tenedor** *nm* fork
tener *vb* to have
yo **tengo** I have (from **tener**)
el **tenis** *nm* tennis
la **terraza** *nf* terrace
testarudo/a *adj* stubborn
la **tía** *nf* aunt
el **tiempo libre** *nm* leisure time
el **tiempo** *nm* weather
la **tienda** *nf* shop
la **tierra** *nf* land
el **tigre** *nm* tiger
tímido/a *adj* shy
el **timo** *nm* scam
el **tío** *nm* uncle
el **tipo** *nm* type
típico/a *adj* typical
tocar *vb* to play (instrument)
todavía *adv* still
todo/a *adj* all
tomar *vb* **el sol** to sunbathe
tonto/a *adj* silly

la **tormenta** *nf* storm
el **toro** *nm* bull
la **tortuga** *nf* tortoise
la **tostada** *nf* piece of toast
lo **traigo** I'll bring it (from **traer**)
el **transporte público** *nm* public transport
travieso/a *adj* naughty
trece thirteen
treinta thirty
el **tren** *nm* train
tres three
tuerce turn (from **torcer**)
turístico/a *adj* touristy

U

por **último** finally
último/a *adj* last
la **universidad** *nf* university
uno one
útil *adj* useful
utilizar *vb* to use

V

la **vaca** *nf* cow
las **vacaciones** *nfpl* holidays
vale la pena it's worth it
el **vampiro** *nm* vampire
los **vaqueros** *nmpl* jeans
variado/a *adj* varied
la **variedad** *nf* variety
el **vaso** *nm* glass
a **veces** *adv* sometimes
veinte twenty
hacer **vela** *vb* to go sailing
la **ventaja** *nf* advantage
la **ventana** *nf* window
ver *vb* to see; to watch
el **verano** *nm* summer

la **verdad** *nf* the truth
verde *adj* green
las **verduras** *nfpl* vegetables
el **vestido (de flamenco)** *nm* (flamenco) dress
vestirse *vb* to get dressed
de **vez en cuando** from time to time
la **vez** *nf* time
viajar *vb* to travel
el **viaje** *nm* journey
los **videojuegos** *nmpl* computer games
viejo/a *adj* old
el **viento** *nm* wind
viernes Friday
el **vino** *nm* (**tinto/blanco**) (red/white) wine
visitar *vb* to visit
vivir *vb* to live
volar *vb* to fly
el **voleibol** *nm* volleyball
volver *vb* to return
yo **voy** I go (from **ir**)
la **vuelta** *nf* tour
vuestro/a *adj* your

Y

y and

Z

las **zapatillas** *nfpl* trainers
los **zapatos** *nmpl* shoes
el **zumo** *nm* juice

OXFORD
UNIVERSITY PRESS

Great Clarendon Street, Oxford OX2 6DP

Oxford University Press is a department of the University of Oxford.

It furthers the University's objective of excellence in research, scholarship, and education by publishing worldwide in

Oxford   New York   Auckland   Cape Town   Dar es Salaam   Hong Kong
Karachi   Kuala Lumpur   Madrid   Melbourne   Mexico City   Nairobi
New Delhi   Shanghai   Taipei   Toronto

With offices in

Argentina   Austria   Brazil   Chile   Czech Republic   France   Greece
Guatemala   Hungary   Italy   Japan   South Korea   Poland   Portugal
Singapore   Switzerland   Thailand   Turkey   Ukraine   Vietnam

Oxford is a registered trade mark of Oxford University Press
in the UK and in certain other countries

British Library Cataloguing in Publication Data

Data available

ISBN 978 019 912754 2

10 9 8 7 6 5 4 3 2

Printed in Malaysia

Paper used in the production of this book is a natural, recyclable product made from wood grown in sustainable forests. The manufacturing process conforms to the environmental regulations of the country of origin.

Acknowledgements

The publishers would like to thank the following for permission to reproduce photographs: p1l-r: Mike Garner/OUP; p4l: Mike Garner/OUP; p4m: Mike Garner/OUP; p4r: Mike Garner/OUP; p5: Mike Garner/OUP; p8tl: Clive Mason/Staff/Getty Images Sport/Getty Images; p8tr: John Rogers/Contributor/Getty Images Entertainment/Getty Images; p8bl: Veniamin Kraskov/Shutterstock; p8br: Amy Nichole Harris/Shutterstock; p9t: Monkey Business Images/Shutterstock; p9ml: Steven May/Alamy; p9mr: Mau Horng/Shutterstock; p9bl: Ivonne Wierink/Shutterstock; p9br: Nito/Shutterstock; p12l: Mike Garner/OUP; p12r: Mike Garner/OUP; p13: Rob Cooke/OUP; p15: quavondo/iStockphoto; p16: Charles Sykes/Rex/Rex Features; p20: OUP; p21: OUP; p22: Regien Paassen/Shutterstock; p22t: Ian Shaw/Alamy; p22b: Dev Carr/Photolibrary; p24tl-tr: Joyce Marrero/Shutterstock, Diego Lezama/Lonely Planet Images/Alamy, Kevin Foy/Rex Features, Hideo Haga/Haga Library; p24ml-mr: Lorenzo Salas/Shutterstock, Eddie Gerald/Alamy, Jborzicchi/Dreamstime, Jasper Juinen/Getty Images News/Getty Images; p24bl-br: John Warburton-Lee Photography/Alamy, EPA/Clickphotos, Jasper Juinen/Staff/Getty Images, Peter Holmes/Photolibrary; p25: OUP; p28t: Mike Garner/OUP; p28ml: Blend Images/Alamy; p28mr: Hola Images/Photolibrary; p28b: Heiner Heine/Photolibrary; p29: Blend Images/Alamy; p31l: Janine Wiedel Photolibrary/Alamy; p31r: Imagebroker Rf/Photolibrary; p35t: David Anthony/Alamy; p35b: Alex Bramwell/Alamy; p36l: Christian Hartmann/Reuters; p36r: Masatoshi Okauchi/Rex Features; p36b: Erik Pendzich/Rex/Rex Features; p37: LatinStock Collection/Alamy; p40tl: Rob Cooke/OUP; p40tr: Rob Cooke/OUP; p40b: OUP; p41t-b: Imagesource/Photolibrary; Adrian Weinbrecht/Photolibrary; Art Directors & TRIP/Alamy; Image Source/Alamy; p43: Robert Fried/Alamy; p44tl: Masterfile; p44tr: Llpo Musto/Rex Features; p44ml: Image Source/Alamy; p44mr: Chris lobina/Alamy; p44bl: Jose Luis Banus-March/Photographer's Choice/Getty images; p44bm: Javier Larrea/Photolibrary; p44br: Crispin Hughes/Photolibrary; p46l: OUP; p46r: Monkey Business Images/Shutterstock; p53t: Design Pics Inc/Photolibrary; p53b: B.O'Kane/Alamy; p54: WH CHOW/Shutterstock; p54lt: Ceredigionpix/Alamy; p54tr: Sugar Gold Images/Photolibrary; p54m: Rob Cooke/OUP; p54b: Lonely Planet Images/Alamy; p57: OUP; p58: OUP; p61t: Mike Garner/OUP; p61b: Heiner Heine/Photolibrary; p63: OUP; p65l: Isabel Alonso de Sudea; p65m: Isabel Alonso de Sudea; p65r: Isabel Alonso de Sudea; p69: sportgraphic/Shutterstock; p70: Rob Cooke/OUP; p72tl: Mogens Trolle/Shutterstock; p72tm: Katja Kreder/Photolibrary; p72tr: Michel Gunther/Photolibrary; p72bl: Vinicius Tupinamba/Dreamstime;

p72bm: Itdarbs/Alamy; p72br: nito/Shutterstock; p74tl-tr: Philip Enticknap/The Travel Library/Photolibrary; David Lyons/Alamy; Andresr/Shutterstock; Hannu Liivaar/Shutterstock; Kevin Wheal/Alamy; p74bl-br: Ondacaracola/Dreamstime, Sokolovsky/Dreamstime, Alex Segre/Rex Features, Obert Obert/Photolibrary, Chris Howes/Wild Places Photography/Alamy; p80tl: Javier Larrea/Photolibrary: p80tm: Pixtal Images/Photolibrary; p80tr: Gardel Bertrand/Photolibrary; p80ml: Luis Castaneda/Photolibrary: p80m: Jose Fuste Raga/Photolibrary: p80mr: Shoosmith Road Works Collection/Alamy; p80bl: Dhoxax/Fotolia; p80br: Lagui/Fotolia; p81: Mike Garner/OUP; p83: Brendan Howard/Shutterstock; p86: Rob Cooke/OUP; p86b: David R. Frazier Photolibrary, Inc./Alamy; p88tl: Bonchan/Shutterstock; p88tr: across/Shutterstock; p88bl: Laure.C/Fotolia; p88bm: Jakub Gojda/Dreamstime; p88br: Pilar Echevarria/Shutterstock; p90tl-tr: FR Images/Alamy, Elaine Smith/Bigstock, Steven May/Alamy, J Marshall-Tribaleye Images/Alamy; P90ml-mr: WaterFrame/Alamy; Chris Ratcliffe/Alamy; Ana Abadía/Photolibrary; Carla Guedes Pinto/Alamy; p90bl-br: Toufikbobo/Fotolia; Edyta Pawlowska/Dreamstime; Elenapavlova/Shutterstock; Success/Fotolia; Robyn Mackenzie/Shutterstock; p90br: OUP; p92l-r: Tim Hill/Alamy; Andalucia Plus Image Bank/Alamy; Antonio Munoz Palomares/Dreamstime; OUP; p96: OUP; p97tl: Pilar Echevarria/Shutterstock; p97tr: ampFotoStudio/Shutterstock; p97bl: Olaf Speier/Shutterstock; p97br: Barbara Pheby/Dreamstime; p102: Thomas La Mela/Shutterstock; p102t: David R. Frazier Photolibrary, Inc./Alamy; p102b: Jacek Chabraszewski/Shutterstock; p104tl-r: Richard Sowersby/Rex Features, Alex Segre/Rex Features, Pakmor/Dreamstime, Norbert Eisele-Hein/Photolibrary; p104bl-br: Richard Sowersby/Rex Features, Tupungato/Dreamstime, Motoring Picture Library/Alamy, Andalucia Plus Image Bank/Alamy; p105: OUP; p106l-r: Elnur Amikishiyev/Bigstock, Europhotos/Alamy, Marc Anderson Photography/Photographers Direct, Imagesource Imagesource/Photolibrary; p108: Deborah Dennis/Alamy; p110: OUP; p111t: Santi Visalli/Photolibrary; p111bl: M.Flynn/Alamy; p111br: Mike Garner/OUP; p113tl-bl: Corey Wise/Lonely Planet Images/Photolibrary, Angelo Cavalli/Photolibrary, Christopher Pillitz/Alamy, Radius Images/Photolibrary; p113tr-br: Fabian von Poser/Photolibrary, Javier Corripio/Alamy; p113bl: Robert Harding Productions/Photolibrary; p113br: Colman Lerner Gerardo/ShutterStock; p116tl: San Rostro/Photolibrary; p116tr: White Star/Monica Gumm/Photolibrary; p116ml: Simon Stacpoole/Rex Features; p116mr: Travelstock44/LOOK-foto/Photolibrary; p116b: Wayne Fogden/Photolibrary; p117l: Greg Balfour Evans/Alamy; P117r: Veniamin Kraskov/Shutterstock; P118t: Alex Segre/Alamy; p118m: Xavier Florensa/Photolibrary; p118: Thomas La Mela/Shutterstock; p118bl: OUP; p118br: OUP; p120tl: Coto Elizondo/The Image Bank/Getty Images; p120tr: Botond/Dreamstime; p120ml-mr: ALCE/Fotolia, Juan Jose Pascual/Photolibrary, Firo Foto/Getty Images Sport/Getty Images, Christian Handl/Photolibrary; p120bl-br: Andrew F. Kazmierski/Shutterstock, The Travel Library/Rex Features, Gonzalo Azumendi/Photolibrary, Visual&Written SL/Alamy; p122tl: Amy Nichole Harris/Shutterstock; p122tr: © 2011 fridakahlo.com; p122b: Mike Garner/OUP; p124l: Lisa F. Young/Shutterstock; p124r: Tracy Whiteside/Shutterstock; p126t: Javier Larrea/Photolibrary; p126r: Rgbspace/Fotolia; p129: Philipp Hympendahl/Alamy; p131t: Hulton Archive/Getty Images; p131m: Adrian Weinbrecht/Photolibrary; p131b: American Honda Motor Co., Inc.; p132tl: Jborzicchi/Dreamstime; p132tr: Susana Vera/Reuters; p132b: Marco Cristofori/Photolibrary; p133t: Jasper Juinen/Getty Images News/Getty images; p133b: Lonni/Shutterstock; p134: OUP; p134b: Goodluz/Shutterstock; p136: Icyimage/Shutterstock; p138: OUP; p140: OUP; p142: Mike Garner/OUP; p147: Mike Garner/OUP; p148t: Rob Cooke/OUP; p148b: Rob Cooke/OUP; p150: Capital Pictures; p152t: Isabel Alonso de Sudea; p152ml: Alexandre Silva/Alamy; p152mr: Olive Images/Photolibrary; p152bl: Blend Images/Alamy; p152br: LMR Group/Alamy; p154tl-tr: Keith Dannemiller/Alamy; Scott Hortop Travel/Alamy; Imagestate Media Partners Limited - Impact Photos/Alamy; Geogre Oze/Alamy; p154ml: PT Images/Shutterstock; p154mr: Ekaterina Monakhova/iStockphoto; p154bl: bikeriderlondon/Shutterstock; p154br: Feverpitch/Shutterstock; p156tl: Andalucia Plus Image Bank/Alamy; p156tr: Matilde Gattoni/Photolibrary; p156m: BUILT Images / Alamy; p156bl: Ambient Ideas/Shutterstock; p156br: Nick Stubbs/Shutterstock; p157tl-bl: Alicia Clarke/Alamy; Mi.Ti./Shutterstock; Riou/photocuisine/Corbis; p157tr-bl: Nito/Shutterstock; pixshots/Shutterstock; Pilar Echevarria/Shutterstock; Dulsita/Fotolia; p158t: Philip Enticknap/The Travel Library/Photolibrary; p158b: Carmen Sedano/Alamy; p159l: David Slater/Alamy; p159r: Hotshotsworldwide/Fotolia.

Illustrations by Kessia Beverley-Smith, Stefan Chabluk, Mark Draisey, Mike Hall, John Hallet, Gemma Hastilow, Lisa Hunt, Scott Jessop, Tim Kahane, Matt Latchford, Victor McLindon, Oxford Designers & Illustrators, Dusan Pavlic, Olivier Prime, Pulsar Studios, Martin Sanders, Ben Swift, Theresa Tibbetts, Laurence Whiteley.

Cover illustration by: Oxford Designers & Illustrators

The authors and publisher would like to thank the following people for their help and advice: Michelle Armstrong, Karen Sherwood.

Audio recordings produced by Colette Thomson for Footstep Productions; Andrew Garratt (engineer).

Video produced by Rob Cooke (director); Mike Garner (cameraman). Actors: Anna Baltasar Galiana (Eva), Anthony Senen Ferra (José), Manu Real Garcia (Khalid) and Juliana Arunategui (Marisa).

Every effort has been made to contact copyright holders of material reproduced in this book. If notified, the publishers will be pleased to rectify any errors or omissions at the earliest opportunity.